Innovative
Governments

Innovative Governments

Creative Approaches to Local Problems

EDITED BY
Douglas J. Watson

 PRAEGER

Westport, Connecticut
London

Library of Congress Cataloging-in-Publication Data

Innovative governments : creative approaches to local problems /
    edited by Douglas J. Watson.
        p. cm.
    Includes bibliographical references and index.
    ISBN 0–275–95515–X (alk. paper)
        1. Local government—United States. 2. State governments—United
    States. 3. Government productivity—United States. I. Watson,
    Douglas J.
    JS341.I56 1997
    350'.000973—dc20   96–33188

British Library Cataloguing in Publication Data is available.

Library of Congress Catalog Card Number: 96–33188
ISBN: 0–275–95515–X

First published in 1997

Praeger Publishers, 88 Post Road West, Westport, CT 06881
An imprint of Greenwood Publishing Group, Inc.

Printed in the United States of America

The paper used in this book complies with the
Permanent Paper Standard issued by the National
Information Standards Organization (Z39.48–1984).

10 9 8 7 6 5 4 3 2

Contents

Contents

Acknowledgments

This book was conceived out of the knowledge that thousands of interesting and innovative approaches to problems are being devised by local governments across the country. Unfortunately, the image of government in the national media has been negative over the past two decades. The editor and contributors to this book decided that we wanted to present examples of how governments are responding to various problems and opportunities. The case studies demonstrate mostly successful attempts at innovative solutions to local problems.

Local governments in the United States are constantly being challenged by their citizens to provide more services with less resources. Since local government-elected and -appointed officials are close to the people they serve, they are held accountable for devising better ways to improve the lives of the people who live in their communities. All but the federal government and the 50 state governments of the more than 83,000 governments in the United States are local governments. The large number of governments and the diverse environments in which they exist provide numerous opportunities for local officials to develop creative solutions to local problems.

Since 1982, I have had the privilege of being the city manager of Auburn, Alabama, a city of approximately 40,000 citizens and the home of Auburn University. During my time as city manager, I have been fortunate to have strong support from City Councilors in the development of an excellent staff of professional public administrators. Many of the contributors to this work are City of Auburn staff members who are recognized leaders in their respective fields. I am grateful to the Auburn elected officials who have created a climate conducive for innovation, and to those public administrators who constantly pursue better ways of providing service to the public.

This book acknowledges the innovative spirit of local government public administrators and elected officials.

Innovative
Governments

1

Climate for Innovation

DOUGLAS J. WATSON

During the decade of the 1990s, there has been constant pressure on government at all levels to be innovative. The critics of government blame government for the ills of society. Much of the criticism has resulted from taxpayers who feel they pay entirely too much of their incomes to government. Many citizens get services that they do not want or ones that governments poorly deliver. The result has been for governments at all levels to respond to this pressure to reform by either downsizing, rightsizing, or reinventing themselves.

Several positive things have come from the pressure on governments to reform. One is the response of government leaders to look at their governments with fresh eyes and question what and why they are doing certain things. Most progressive governments, especially on the local level, have developed mission statements that focus on what the government is doing to address its most essential tasks. This approach gives elected and appointed officials the opportunity to question whether what they are doing still makes sense in this anti-government era. They can deemphasize or eliminate those functions that are not central to their mission.

A second development is the recognized need to do more with less. Citizens in most communities will not stand for increased taxes, nor will they stand for fewer services. The result is that government leaders are forced to develop new approaches to providing services. Some of these efforts at finding better ways of doing things have worked and some have not been successful.

Third, many of the roles that local governments assumed in the past three decades were not their traditional ones but ones the federal or state governments mandated to them. In addition, the courts, both federal and state, have placed many new responsibilities on local governments as the individual rights of citizens have expanded over the past 20 years. As a result, local governments have had to learn to adjust to accommodate these new responsibilities.

In attempting to adjust to these legislative and judicial mandates, government leaders have had to be involved in programs and services that were unheard of only two decades ago. For example, many local governments have created risk management programs or departments to identify problems that could result in monetary losses if litigated. Those problems may be in employment practices, employee safety, infrastructure condition, and numerous other possibilities, sometimes too isolated to imagine until they develop.

Fourth, the management of local governments has become significantly better trained and more professional in its approach to solving problems and service delivery than in the past. While educational achievement does not necessarily result in improved service delivery, it does indicate that better-trained people are now assuming management roles in local government. Many of these professionals are seeking better ways of providing services and encouraging their governments to face problems that confront communities.

CONDITIONS FOR INNOVATION

Certain conditions have to exist in local government for innovation to flourish:

1. *Organizational culture.* A culture that supports and encourages innovation is essential. The first and probably the foremost barrier to innovation is a culture that rewards those who maintain the status quo. Robert Behn noted that "in the public sector the dominant measure of success is not the achievement of goals. It is

not getting accused of doing anything wrong." If this is the case, then there is little chance that a local government will undertake any innovative programs or policies.

Managers have a responsibility to direct the development of an organizational culture that encourages innovation and that rewards managers who are innovative. Innovation requires some risk. If managers are to be innovative, they must be willing to take risks. If they fear punishment should they fail, then they are not likely to risk innovation.

2. *Political support.* Public administrators need to have support from elected officials. Wise elected officials know that there is some risk in innovation, and they need to tolerate an occasional failure. Retaining one's job may become the main purpose that a manager has in life if his or her job is threatened politically. It is very unlikely that such a manager will be innovative under these circumstances. In addition, if the elected officials are in constant disagreement, a manager may be hesitant to risk proposing an innovative idea out of fear that it will be politicized.

3. *Administrative competence.* Many local governments have managers, such as department heads, who have vested interests in keeping things the way they are. If an innovation results in removing a function from a manager through consolidation or privatization, the manager ideally should determine his or her support for or opposition to it based on what is best for the city or county for which he or she works. Often, the manager bases his or her response on what the innovation may do to his or her power base, not whether it is good for the community. It is the job of the mayor or city manager to encourage innovation by adjusting the attitudes of those department managers who are mainly interested in the size of their budgets.

Innovation in government generally takes place under one of three scenarios. The first scenario that produces innovation is response to a crisis. Shakespeare said, "Sweet are the uses of adversity." Local governments often have a mandate to cause substantial change in reaction to adversity. Often governments find that the status quo is difficult to change under normal circumstances because elected and appointed officials have no incentive to change. "We've always done it that way before" becomes the slogan for anyone who does not want to change the way a government is delivering services or handling routine problems. However, when a crisis develops and the way "we've always done it" does not work any more, governments are forced to find a better way to solve the problem, or they will fail. Generally, failure results in the removal of appointed officials and possibly the loss in the next election of the elected officials who failed to foresee and handle the crisis.

Examples of innovation resulting from overcoming adversity are to be found everywhere, and many may be relatively simple in design. For example, a public works director establishes a literacy training program when he realizes that his truck drivers cannot read the street name signs in the city where they are working. A second example is the establishment by a police chief of a bicycle patrol to combat drug traffic because the drug dealers can spot the police patrol cars easily and can stop their illegal activity long enough for the cruiser to move past them. A third example is a risk manager who develops a self-funded workers compensation program when the premiums through normal insurance channels become prohibitive.

The second scenario is the existence within a local government of exceptional managers who have the political support to be innovative. Enlightened elected officials expect the local government to do the best job that it can do and are willing to be limited risk takers. The elected officials and the top appointed officials encourage innovation throughout the organization and reward employees and managers who are innovative. Rather than feeling threatened by innovation, organizations like this celebrate innovation by accepting the risk that may come with an innovation and praising the innovator.

Examples of encouraging innovation by organizations also are found in many local governments. For example, cities that undertake curbside recycling programs because they believe they have a responsibility to society to reuse valuable materials are innovative. A second example is affordable housing programs for low- and moderate-income citizens in partnership with the private sector. Another example is a police chief who establishes a citizen police academy to involve citizens in the difficult job of providing law enforcement to the community.

The third scenario that produces innovation is found in organizations that recognize and seize opportunities when they see them. Unless an organization is prepared to try new ways of addressing problems, it is unlikely that it will even recognize an opportunity to be innovative. Public administrators need support from elected officials. If elected officials are at odds with each other or with the administrators, the environment within the organization is not conducive for innovation.

Local governments with innovative organizational cultures are ones that seize opportunities when they arise. For example, cities that established revolving loan funds with recovered federal funds from programs of the 1970s and the 1980s now have the capacity to engage in proactive economic development efforts. Other cities spent their recovered funds or allowed developers to default on the loans and lost them. Another example is a local government that consolidates its emergency medical services with a local hospital when the hospital decides to move aggressively into the ambulance business. A third example is cities that privatized their water and wastewater facilities in the 1980s before the Tax Reform Act. The tax law from 1981 to 1986 allowed significant savings for local governments that privatized the construction of new facilities.

THE REST OF THE BOOK

This book will present a number of case studies that illustrate a few of the innovations that are taking place in local governments across the country. The case studies cover a broad array of local government programs and services. They demonstrate that innovation is possible in any service produced by government as long as innovation is encouraged by the organizational culture, there is strong political support for innovation, and there are competent administrators who can develop and implement new approaches and programs. Quality government through innovation is not only possible, but essential, in all of the services and programs of local government, as these case studies indicate.

The first case study (Chapter 2) is the story of a coastal Florida county that realized that its most precious natural resource (water) was being misused, causing numerous problems for its residents. Through careful building of community support and hard work of competent administrators, the county was able to devise and implement a comprehensive stormwater plan that resulted in viewing stormwater as a resource to be carefully managed rather than simply removed from land as quickly as possible. An important part of this innovation was the establishment of stormwater management as a separate utility, with the residents charged an annual fee for stormwater service based on the extent of their contribution to the cost of controlling it.

The second case study (Chapter 3) relates the story of a university community, faced with accelerating population growth, developing innovative solutions to two public safety challenges. The first innovation was the creation of a student firefighter program that supplemented the career firefighters and reduced manpower costs by two-thirds. In addition, the program provided financial resources for college students to work their way through college while serving the city in which they lived. The second innovation describes the process by which the city proposed and achieved the consolidation of its emergency medical service with the ambulance service of the community hospital despite the opposition of firefighters and paramedics. In this case, the city saved over $1 million during the first seven years of the consolidated program.

The third case study (Chapter 4) describes the difficult situation faced by a mid-size Florida city in the mid-1980s when insurance premiums soared despite the city's excellent loss history. In response to the crisis of skyrocketing prices for insurance, the city's leaders cooperatively developed a self-funded risk management program that has saved the city millions of dollars over the past decade. Administrative competence coupled with strong political support for the innovation led to a highly successful implementation of the risk management program.

The fourth case study (Chapter 5) involves a city that faced industrial, commercial, and residential growth in the early 1980s with an antiquated zoning ordinance. There was consensus in the community that the quality of development was sorely lacking, and citizens expected the city council to adopt progressive legislation that would require developers to meet higher standards. The result was the adoption of a performance zoning ordinance with very stringent development standards. This innovative approach to land use controls led to a disruptive debate in the community that involved developers, land owners, and neighborhood associations.

Excellent staff work and strong political leadership led to the successful adoption and implementation of the zoning law that has improved significantly the quality of development in the community over the past decade.

The fifth case study (Chapter 6) describes a city's acceptance of a proactive role in providing housing for its low- and moderate-income residents. It is a role that apathetic appointed and elected leaders would not have undertaken. The result has been an award-winning affordable housing program that has improved the quality of life in the city for a number of residents. In addition, it demonstrates how the public and private sectors can work together to address community problems when the public sector takes the lead and assumes risk and responsibility. The response to the housing shortage for low- and moderate-income citizens involves political leadership, competent administrators, and adversity created by a failing housing stock.

The sixth case study (Chapter 7) tells the story of a small city that was facing unprecedented expansion of its boundaries through annexation of its urbanized fringe. The elected officials of the community realized that a new approach to governing was needed to cope with the changes that were occurring, and changed the form of government. While not an innovation by national standards, the adoption of council-manager government was a bold innovation for this community. Unfortunately, the effort to be innovative was not carefully researched nor implemented and resulted in failure. For innovators in government, there are important lessons contained in this case study. The first is to consider carefully all of the factors that may doom the innovation to failure. The second is to build support for it among those who have the ability to determine its success or failure. The third is to conceive a plan for implementation that considers as many factors as possible. And lastly, it is important that competent administrators be hired with the experience and ability to implement the innovation.

CONCLUSION

It is a difficult time to be a public administrator. Trust in government at all levels appears to be at an all-time low. If government is not being reinvented, it is being reengineered, reformed, or right-sized. Critics of government exist at every level of government and at every point on the political spectrum. To a large degree, confidence can be restored in government if public administrators will search for innovative solutions to the pressing problems facing their communities. One of the ways this can be done is through efficiency (i.e., doing more with less). The other is through effectiveness (i.e., doing better what we are now doing not so well). The case studies in this book illustrate attempts, some successful and one not successful, of local governments to be innovative.

2

Managing Stormwater in a Coastal Community

RONALD W. McLEMORE AND
T. DUNCAN ROSE, III

For many years, stormwater management has been a peripheral or secondary responsibility of the "public works" function in most local governments. The various elements that comprise a comprehensive stormwater management program are typically scattered throughout a city's or county's governmental organization. Indeed, most attention at the local level in Florida has been directed to building and maintaining roads, sewer systems, and water plants and to controlling snowballing traffic in the struggle to address the often overwhelming forces of growth.

However, most Florida jurisdictions are learning that relegating stormwater management to a backseat role comes at a substantial price. Accumulating pollution, deteriorating rivers and estuaries, drinking water problems, state and federal regulation and, most pointedly, the flood reminders of recent major storms throughout Florida have pushed stormwater management out of its secondary role and into the limelight.

To address adequately the complex, interwoven issues that form the context of stormwater management requires an innovative organizational vehicle, one which focuses management direction and fiscal resources solely on executing an effective stormwater program. A stormwater utility is the organizational vehicle selected by many jurisdictions in Florida and across the nation to deliver the stormwater management program. Successful development and implementation of a utility is difficult. It requires a careful integration of political, technical, and organizational strategies. It also requires creativity and innovation in the design of a fair, legally defensible, and technically valid rate structure. But above all, it requires identifying, and taking timely advantage of, all the windows of opportunity contained within the political and institutional environment.

This study focuses on the interaction between certain key "breakthrough" structural innovations designed into the fabric of a stormwater utility for Martin County, Florida, and the "strategical opportunity space" which those innovations created, ultimately opening the doors to political and community acceptance of the program.

THE COMMUNITY CONTEXT

For millions of years, the various physical forces of nature have shaped and fine-tuned the physiological systems that make Martin County the beautiful and bountiful area that it is. The county, composed of 542 square miles, ranges some 21 miles along the Atlantic coast, just east of the Lake Okeechobee/Everglade natural systems. Large coastal dune systems, the Indian River Lagoon, the St. Lucie River and Estuary, the coastal uplands, the large glade wetland plain, the western uplands, and finally the Everglade system itself all interweave to form one of the richest and most complex ecological systems on earth. At the heart of these forces of nature is water—water as rainfall, standing in wetlands, stored in aquifers, rivers, creeks, estuary; water above, in, on, and below ground. Water so essential that, by its quantity, quality, location, and duration, it determines the very communities of life in Martin County.

The richness and diversity of Martin County's ecosystems are both boon and bane: without careful management, population growth and attendant land development threaten to overwhelm the fragile structure on which it is founded. Nowhere is this more pertinent than in stormwater management.

Seventy-five years of increasingly intensive land development has provided homes, economic opportunity, and vacation enjoyment for hundreds of thousands of people. But this same influx of residents and visitors has exacted a toll on the water-based physiological systems which for millennia have cycled and stored rainwater in wetland, soil, aquifer, and river. Without systematic management, Martin County stands to diminish irretrievably this critical resource.

Martin County was created in 1925 from the southern portion of St. Lucie County and the northern portion of Palm Beach County. The county was famous in the early 1900s as a producer of pineapples. In later years, it was dubbed the sailfish capital of the world, which reflects its long history as a sportfishing and commercial fishing area. While the county experienced several "almost" real estate booms, it remained relatively undeveloped until 1960. Since 1960, the county has experienced significant growth, increasing in population from 16,942 to 100,900 in 1990. While the coastal area of the county has a mixture of old Florida and new urban form, the western half of the county (to lake Okeechobee) is still primarily agricultural in nature.

STORMWATER AND THE PUBLIC AGENDA

During a Board of County Commissioners' retreat in autumn 1992, the board identified stormwater management as a top priority for the future. The county staff prepared three reports over the course of two years that mapped out a strategy for developing and funding a systematic and comprehensive stormwater management program for a 10-year period for both operational services and capital improvements.

The first report presented background information about the causes and effects of stormwater in Martin County. The report also provided a summary of stormwater regulations within Martin County and a comparison to the regulations of other jurisdictional entities within the county, particularly the South Florida Water Management District (SFWMD). Common problems associated with insufficient stormwater management were discussed, including environmental degradation and lack of comprehensive planning. The current and future direction of the county's stormwater program was addressed, including intergovernmental coordination

with the SFWMD, adjacent St. Lucie County, the Indian River Lagoon National Estuary Program, and others.

Following a workshop in which the first report was presented
and discussed, the board directed the county staff to prepare a
long-range (10–year) stormwater master plan outlining goals and
projects necessary to meet those goals within the county. This master plan, the second report presented to the board, focused on identifying programs, projects, activities, and related costs to
implement a comprehensive stormwater management plan to reduce the negative impacts of untreated stormwater on the county's
water resources.

The third and final report comprising the Martin County stormwater program was presented to the board on June 28, 1994. It
included alternatives for financing the projects identified in the 10-
year stormwater master plan project/program element, which was
the second report to the board. This report also presented a revised
program listing that included approximately $18 million in various
capital projects to address the goals and concerns of the St. Lucie
Initiative, a local, politically prominent environmental group. It
included an additional $1 million for operation and maintenance
of existing privately maintained stormwater facilities that the
county planned to acquire. County staff reviewed possible revenue
sources including general fund revenues, dedicated sales and property taxes, special assessments, and stormwater utility fees. The
result of this review was the recommendation to pursue a utility-
based system using annual assessments as its revenue source.

In the summer of 1994, the county staff recommended retention
of a consulting team to review the staff proposals, to make recommendations, and to devise an implementation plan with county
staff. Work on Phase 1 of the effort commenced in November
1994.

County's Strategy

Retaining consultant expertise was only one component of the
county's developmental strategy. Many different actors and many
different agendas would have to be integrated into a carefully administered process if the implementation of the utility was to be
successful.

The county's strategy was built around three components: (1) a technical team, called the steering team, composed of county staff; engineering, legal, and systems consultant expertise; and local civil engineers; (2) a citizen task force composed of 17 residents appointed by the county commission and selected to represent interests in the community most affected by the program; and (3) the Board of County Commissioners and senior management staff.

The steering team was charged with reviewing the staff's proposed stormwater management program and with developing a rate structure that implemented both the operations and capital portions of the program. It was critical that the structure meet stringent Florida law governing assessments. The citizen task force was to serve as a sounding board to test the recommendations of the steering team against the realities of community perception.

Engineering Community

Where there is development, either agricultural or urban in nature, civil engineers are needed to provide professional expertise in reshaping the face of the land to accommodate the developmental intent. In Martin County, three separate, major local governmental entities regulate the land development process and the engineers who design within the body of regulations:

1. the city of Stuart and other chartered communities for development within their jurisdictions;

2. the county for development outside the chartered city and towns; and

3. the South Florida Water Management District, which has statutory regulatory control over all waters of the state and water flowing into them.

Over the years, in an effort to simplify the regulatory environment, many communities have adopted the water management district's regulatory requirements as their own local development code, adding a few refinements as applicable. Historically, the water management district's rules have been more restrictive than those of local jurisdictions. This, however, was not the case in Martin County. Historically, Martin County has had an extremely restrictive view of growth. The intentional posture of politically strong members of the community has been to limit growth through regulation and by denial of development orders for rezoning to higher-intensity use.

For some 20 years, the county has utilized a "pre/post" rule for stormwater system design that is one of the most restrictive in the state. While most jurisdictions have a "pre/post" rule (which stipulates that the runoff coming from a parcel cannot leave the property at a *rate* greater than the rate at which it moved prior to the development), Martin's rule is far more encompassing. It stipulates that the "discharged volume, flow, timing and quality of stormwater in the post-developed condition shall be approximately the same as pre-development."

Martin County's provision is substantially more restrictive than the current SFWMD requirements. Thus, while a permit for development can be obtained from the SFWMD for a given design, that design may require additional information and/or redesign to meet county requirements. The additional requirements frustrated the local engineering community to the point that real tension existed among staff, the commission, and the local engineers. At issue were the interpretation of the rules, how the rules were to be met, why the county felt it necessary to take this approach, and the extra design costs often necessary to obtain a permit.

The St. Lucie River Initiative

In 1990, a group of citizens, deeply concerned about the future of the St. Lucie River and estuary, organized a not-for-profit organization called the St. Lucie River Initiative. The group's objective was to identify all issues related to the health and vitality of the river, to identify what organizations had responsibility for resolving those issues, and to pursue appropriate remedies with those organizations. Because stormwater plays such a key role in the physiological process at work in the river, stormwater management, especially quality-related retrofit of site facilities, is a major issue with the initiative. With a membership of over 1,200 local residents, most of whom are well-educated, articulate, and highly motivated, the organization has significant impact on local politics.

The organization maintains a positive but skeptical view of government's capability to address the improvement of the river.

Stormwater Problems Facing the County

The county's steering team identified four substantial stormwater management challenges facing Martin County. Three are functional in nature:

1. *Flooding.* Flooding problems within Martin County range in severity from standing water on lawns and driveways for short periods of time, to home inundation, to septic system failure and its associated adverse health risks.

2. *Water quality.* Three distinct water quality issues have been identified within Martin County by various sources. Large freshwater inputs during flood conditions and a lack of freshwater during low-flow conditions cause portions of the estuary to alternate between freshwater and very salty conditions. The quality of the water column has deteriorated in some areas due to excessive nutrients, heavy metal, and organics (petroleum distillates and, to some extent, pesticides) input from urban and agricultural runoff. Flocculent sediments, clay, and silt are accumulating (or have accumulated) on portions of the estuary bottom.

3. *Water supply and conservation.* The water supply for public, business, agricultural, and environmental use in Martin County is threatened by loss of surface storage, hazardous materials contamination, and salt water intrusion into the drinking aquifer. This issue is complex, is not entirely a stormwater management problem, and involves a wide spectrum of efforts including conservation strategies.

These three functional problems are compounded by a fourth, historically based problem:

4. *Incremental, disjointed stormwater system.* The county's stormwater facilities and systems were sized and installed incrementally over the years with little information available to the designers about existing basin conditions and less about future needs. Consequently, the system is a series of stand-alone subsystems with little consideration as to how each relates to the others. Even under impact from moderate-size storms, the existing system quickly

reaches its limits. It is far from adequately addressing the increasing challenges placed on it.

AN EMERGING SOLUTION

These four stormwater management challenges were not insurmountable. The sooner practical steps were taken, however, the lower the long-term cost of implementing the solutions would be, and the faster stability would be returned to the riverine and estuary ecological systems. Most importantly, the rate at which critical water resources would be irreversibly lost to salt intrusion would be substantially reduced. The problem was how to coalesce the community around a solution. Just what should the solution be? And how could it be funded in an era of anti–government program sentiment?

A Policy of Integration

The key to a successful strategy was integration of innovative stormwater engineering strategies with other community strategies for building facilities or programs that may not be directly or entirely related to stormwater management. Needs for community park facilities, preservation of water recharge areas, reclaimed water reuse, greenbelts, wildlife and conservation areas and corridors, and preservation of wetlands, rivers, creeks, and the estuary had to be folded into the long-term stormwater management strategy to stretch each dollar invested by the county.

Most importantly, stormwater had to be recognized as something more than a short-term engineering problem; it constitutes a resource critical to the sustenance of the urban community and the biological community alike. Since each community is inextricably linked to the welfare of the other, a successful program had to balance the impact of the management of this resource between the urban and natural communities.

Traditionally, stormwater has been viewed as a bothersome irritant in the urban and agricultural land development process. The objective has been to rid the surface of the water quickly by routing it directly into creeks, wetlands, ponds, and rivers. Such practices, as south Florida has learned, have a dramatic impact on the physiological systems at work in the area. Soils that once stored large volumes of water for long periods of time are deprived of water. Rather than creeping across large wetland prairies at slow rates, stormwater is conveyed rapidly into receiving bodies at specific points. The negative effect on the physiological systems is substantial and ultimately large scale. Rather than being cleaned by biological processes in the creep across the plains, stormwater is channeled with a higher concentration of contaminants into nonbiological conveyance systems that then pass runoff in large quantity at focused points into receiving bodies. Subsurface systems, once replenished in this creep across the plains, are now deprived of the water, and its attendant backpressure, so necessary to hold back the saltwater pressing in from the weight of the ocean.

Effective stormwater management builds upon the concept of multiple use as its key strategic component. Providing adequate stormwater storage and conveyance can go hand-in-hand with providing greenbelts, parks, reservoirs, and conservation areas. Effective stormwater and conveyance systems can be fully integrated with reclaimed water programs to concentrate on effective recharge of the aquifer and provision of irrigation for agriculture and lawn maintenance. These same tactics lead to biological treatment of contaminants that in turn leads to stability of the ecosystem and reduced degradation of receiving bodies. Finally, an integrated approach achieves a salinity management program that preserves a consistent salinity range necessary to a stable estuary.

An effective stormwater management program views stormwater not as something to be disposed of as quickly as possible, but rather as a resource that needs to be carefully managed. Ineffective management leads to flooding, pollution, and salt incursion into the drinking aquifer; effective management strikes an appropriate balance between the needs of nature and the needs of the urban community.

THE STORMWATER MANAGEMENT PROGRAM

The county's plan, as presented in the staff's second report, contains six programs: data management, operations and maintenance, capital projects, development services, regulation, and administration.

Data management. The data management program consists of the collection, inventory, manipulation, and dissemination of all data related to stormwater management and water quality within the county. Data are collected on existing drainage structures and facilities, rainfall, flow rates, groundwater levels, water quality, topography, and other mapping information. These data are inventoried and manipulated using the county's geographic information system (GIS) and other systems to assess the state of existing water resources, identify trends, and predict the state of future water resources. Computer modeling using hydrologic and hydraulic analysis of the county's water resources is included within this section of the plan. These data are then made available to the public to encourage public education and to coordinate improvement efforts.

Operation and maintenance (O&M). The operation and maintenance program is divided into three sections and consists of the inspection, cleaning, grading, mowing, and replacement of stormwater conveyance and storage facilities in disrepair. Part one of the program consists of the routine maintenance required to provide uninhibited stormwater conveyance and to prevent county-maintained stormwater facilities from becoming unsightly. Part two identifies activities to maintain the health of man-made wetlands through exotic and nuisance vegetation removal. Part three lists "special" individual projects designed to solve minor flooding problems utilizing existing manpower over the next few years.

Capital projects. The capital projects program identifies areas proposed for water quality and flood protection improvement. Approximately 15 drainage areas are listed, with brief descriptions of proposed improvements such as culvert replacement, new culvert installations, and retention/detention facility construction, as well as experimental projects on marsh flow-ways and fertilizer mixing facilities. Some of these project areas were selected because they were identified in the Martin County growth management plan as level of service deficiencies, while others were identified in various reports performed for the county as a result of citizen complaints.

One important item discussed in the third report to the board was the revised stormwater management master program costs. During the period between the second and third reports, the program costs were revised to reflect increases resulting from a new service area being added to O&M, increases in operating expenses from revised budget estimates, revisions to capital projects costs, and additional capital projects to address concerns of the St. Lucie Initiative task force. By far, the largest increase in program costs was for capital costs for the St. Lucie retrofit projects. These projects were identified to provide pre-treatment of stormwater runoff prior to entering the St. Lucie estuary for all developed areas within the county constructed prior to 1979 (before regulations requiring stormwater treatment were implemented). Approximately 79 individual project areas were identified.

Following the presentation of the third report to the board, county staff continued to refine the "special" maintenance, capital, and St. Lucie retrofit projects and compiled a single listing in March 1995 of all proposed projects. This list contained three categories of projects: capital and original special O&M projects, O&M projects as a result of tropical storm Gordon, and St. Lucie retrofit projects. The list included refinements to project areas to eliminate project duplication.

With the completion of the review by the consulting members of the steering team, the needed programs and general capital projects had been identified. What remained was the formidable task of devising a funding structure which the community would accept as fair and reasonable.

Development services. The development services program formalizes and augments plan and site review of public and private development projects.

Regulation. The regulation program has three major functions: (1) promulgation and revision of stormwater regulations; (2) compliance monitoring; and (3) enforcement of stormwater regulations. This program dedicates staff for these functions in order to further protect the county's water resources.

Administration. The administration program has two main responsibilities: (1) program/project management; and (2) intergovernmental coordination.

The program/project management element includes the efforts of the county administration in the areas of direction, organization, construction management, and accountability. This element includes the management of all programs and capital projects except O&M activities. However, the administration of right-of-way acquisition for O&M activities is included in this element. The function of the intergovernmental element is the coordination of numerous governmental entities, special interest groups, and the general public with regard to water resource issues. The purpose of this coordination is the acquisition of grant monies, accurate dissemination of information, accurate representation of county interests in regional issues, technical support to groups working within the county, consensus building to provide a basis for action, and public education.

THE FUNDING STRUCTURE: TOWARD A STORMWATER UTILITY

Like all utilities, a stormwater utility has two fundamental structural characteristics: it is a defined organizational entity charged with accountability for a specific program, and it is a stand-alone, self-contained accounting entity with defined revenues and restricted expenditures.

Organizational Entity

As an organizational entity, a stormwater utility has a mission or purpose to provide a defined level of stormwater management service to the community. It is provided financial resources and charged with the management of human resources and of the support equipment necessary for those personnel to effectively and efficiently accomplish the mission.

As an organizational entity, a stormwater utility can pursue one of two courses in providing services: it can contract with other units within the city or county organizational structure (such as public works road maintenance personnel) to provide services, or it can acquire its own staff and provide services directly. In either event, the fundamental objective of the organizational aspect of a utility is the clear assignment of accountability. Final responsibility for performance in achieving the stormwater program objectives lies with the utility structure.

Martin County staff identified a full range of stormwater management services typically provided by a full-service utility: administration; operations and maintenance; regulation and development review; quality monitoring (water bodies); performance inspection (existing facilities); system planning and modeling (regional and basin level); system design; facilities construction; and construction inspection (new facilities).

Accounting Entity

The second fundamental characteristic of a utility is its stand-alone accounting entity status. Consistent with Generally Accepted Accounting Practices, the stormwater utility must be structured as either a special revenue fund or an enterprise fund. Such fund designation requires that revenues generated by or transferred to the utility be spent solely for legitimate stormwater management functions.

Special revenue fund designation provides for the isolation of revenues and expenditures appropriate to the utility concept. Its set-up requirements are simple; hence, it has substantial appeal as a funding mechanism. Enterprise fund designation brings additional obligations of asset valuation and the preparation of various financial statements not required of a special revenue fund. However, such designation also clearly establishes the organizational integrity of the utility.

Reasons for a Stormwater Utility

Martin County identified two reasons for creating a stormwater utility: program focus and equity of cost. The program focus aspect recognizes the management principle that an organization tends to focus its attention on those programs for which it is clearly organized to deliver. An organization accountable for and organized to deliver stormwater management services will tend to deliver the stormwater management services better than one charged primarily with other objectives and to which the stormwater function is attached as a secondary objective.

A fundamental concept of any utility is the capacity of the service delivered by that utility to be bought in measurable, discrete units of service. Hence, electricity is purchased in kilowatt hours, phone service in minutes of service connect time, water in thousands of gallons, and so forth. In each case, the buyer pays only for what he or she consumes. This concept is founded on the intuitively appealing notion that one pays proportionately to the cost or burden one puts on the system.

Typically, stormwater programs are funded from gas tax revenue or general fund revenue, which in Florida comes primarily from sales tax and property tax. Here, in effect, one's share of stormwater program costs is related to how much gas one buys, how much one spends at the mall, or the value of one's property rather than how much stormwater runoff one's property generates.

By incorporating this "causer of cost" concept, a market incentive is generated at the property-owner level to reduce stormwater contribution to avoid the costs associated with the management of the runoff. Rather than a regulatory burden, privately owned mitigation facilities (stormwater management systems and facilities on site that reduce the rate, amount, or pollutant load of runoff) become economically attractive, as does the timely maintenance of those facilities, since provision for and maintenance of private "runoff reducing" facilities trigger a substantial credit on the stormwater bill.

Rationale for a Rate Structure

Consistent with earlier staff recommendations, the consultant team recommended imposition of an assessment to fund the stormwater management program. The assessment rate structure was developed from the standpoint of legal "defensibility," the soundness of its structural logic, and its fairness to all affected customers.

Several fundamental questions had to be addressed in the development of the stormwater assessment rate structure: (1) how to bill equitably all parcels that generate stormwater runoff—residential, commercial, industrial, agricultural, and undeveloped parcels; (2) how to apportion program costs fairly to each parcel; (3) how to bill for services or capital improvements projects that may serve only a portion of the county; and (4) how to make residential parcel billing equitable yet simple.

While many legal tenets pertain to the imposition of an assessment in Florida, two broad fundamental principles must be considered. First, each parcel assessed must receive a special benefit (e.g., the removal of the burden each parcel creates upon a stormwater management system); and second, the costs of the services and facilities provided must be fairly and reasonably apportioned among the benefited parcels.

Only those parcels that receive a special benefit from the stormwater management program can be assessed for the service and/or capital costs expended. Parcels that can currently be construed as receiving special benefit are those that are hydrologically connected (directly or indirectly) to an existing or proposed county stormwater facility, and/or those within a hydrologically defined area, such as a basin where the county implements a comprehensive capital projects program to correct existing deficiencies.

Finally, parcels not hydrologically connected may also be construed to receive special benefit through a "transfer of burden" (i.e., where parcels that are being treated are treated at a higher level to compensate for those for which treatment is not financially feasible).

Both "how much" and "to where" stormwater flows are key components of this burden concept; a parcel's share of the stormwater burden (costs incurred by the county to manage runoff) is proportionately related to the relative amount of runoff generated by a parcel. Conversely, stormwater runoff that does not eventually flow to a county-maintained system, or does not otherwise constitute a burden of runoff to the county, is no more chargeable than electricity not consumed or telephone calls not made by those utilities. This concept underscores the special benefit nature of this theory—the benefit to a parcel varies proportionately with the burden passed to the county; parcels differently situated with respect to runoff benefit differently.

Since the calculation of stormwater runoff is a clearly defined engineering science, the rate structure should replicate in a highly simplified form the approach a stormwater engineer would apply in reviewing a parcel. Assigning a bill amount to a specific parcel is accomplished in two steps:

1. *Cost apportionment.* Costs of each service rendered and each capital project implemented by the utility must be carefully and separately identified. The geographic range of each of these services or capital projects must be carefully defined on a county map. These services or capital projects are either county-wide, multi-basin, basin-wide, or sub-basin in nature.

2. *Parcel apportionment.* The "geographically" specific costs

identified above are subsequently apportioned to each eligible parcel using an engineering-based approach that assesses the impact on runoff of pervious and impervious area; a parcel's area in ponds, lakes, and wetlands; its topography (whether the parcel drains to a county facility); and the presence or absence of mitigating systems such as retention and detention facilities.

To simplify the billing approach, rate classes are used where feasible. Bills are rendered to the parcel owner measured in terms of equivalent stormwater units (ESUs). An ESU is defined as the relative stormwater runoff generated by a "typical" single-family residence in Martin County. The value is determined based on statistical sampling.

Single-family residences (SFRs) are broken into three single-family residential classes, depending upon lot size, and billed one of three fees accordingly. Most SFRs are billed one ESU. The largest one-fourth of SFR parcels are billed proportionately more; the smallest one-fourth are billed proportionately less. Apartments and condominiums are assessed based on the ESUs associated with the complex.

ESUs for non-single-family residential parcels (commercial, institutional, industrial, agricultural, vacant, and so forth) are determined based on site-specific characteristics such as the size of the parcel, the amount of hard or impervious area on the parcel, the nature of the soft or pervious cover, certain characteristics of the soil, and the parcel's composition of lakes, ponds, and wetlands. Substantial credit is given for the presence on site of privately owned stormwater "mitigation" facilities. Agricultural and undeveloped land are assessed on the same basis as other non-residential property, but assessors use a broader range of "pervious coefficients" (natural state, pasture, groves, row crops, and so forth) to estimate more accurately relative runoff for parcels with large pervious area.

A TWO-STAGED IMPLEMENTATION STRATEGY

The consultant team recommended a two-staged implementation of the stormwater assessment. Certain key data that are necessary to the implementation of a full assessment system require time to build and validate. Billing cycle one, scheduled for November

1995, entailed a flat charge per parcel throughout the unincorporated county area. The flat charge per parcel was predicated on the need to determine from map-based data which parcels are inside the various benefit areas and which parcels are outside the benefit areas. The amount of the first-year charge was set by the county commission based on anticipated costs for the data analysis and other program costs. This rate was set at $9.75 per parcel.

Revenue from this assessment funded the building of the data bases, the initial parcel review process, and the development of the billing calculation system necessary to implement the full assessment methodology. In addition, a portion of the revenues funded development of a master system plan that guides the determination of levels of service for each hydrologic area, and coordinates detailed basin studies to identify deficiencies within the given level of service.

Billing cycle two, scheduled for November 1996, incorporated the data and program development to implement fully the stormwater management and assessment program. The cost per ESU was to be set by the county commission at that time. Typically, cities and counties across the state that have implemented utility fees or assessments have set rates ranging from $35 to $60 per year per single-family residence to cover operating costs. Capital costs vary much more widely in those few areas that have developed capital programs as part of the implementation stage.

PUBLIC INFORMATION PROGRAM

An informed public is essential to implementing successfully the stormwater management program and assessment rate structure. Virtually every major jurisdiction in the state and across the country that has successfully implemented a stormwater utility points to a successful public information program as a key. The public information strategy must be practical and thrifty. It must focus on clearly communicating what the problems with the current approach are, why it is important to address them now, how the problems are expected to be resolved, how much it is expected to cost, and how it will be funded.

The information program in Martin County was built around four strategies:

1. The maintenance of the technical committee of local civil engineers who met regularly with county staff and the consulting team to review the county's stormwater management program and emerging projects list.

2. Inclusion of the South Florida Water Management District staff on the technical committee to assure communication about and influence in determining SFWMD studies and capital projects, and to maintain a close coordination with district projects, studies, and emerging regulatory modification.

3. Recommissioning of the citizen review committee as a standing advisory committee.

4. Execution of a broadly focused information program that incorporates a range of public informational tools, such as video tape, public service announcements, newspaper supplements, mailers, and civic presentations. The citizen review committee was established to assist in "placing the stormwater management program on the public agenda." Its role is to review the articulated issues list; suggest additions, modifications, and deletions to the stormwater program; and provide a sounding board for review of the proposed solutions. In addition, it serves as a source for disseminating information to the community. It was not intended to be a final decision-making authority or a technical committee. It informs residents and property owners of the nature and magnitude of the stormwater management challenges facing Martin County, of the general strategy for addressing much of the problem, and of specific plans for each basin/benefit area within the county. Finally, it advises how the assessment is levied and what the magnitude of the expected assessments are.

THE WINDOWS OF OPPORTUNITY

The process leading to the building of the stormwater utility in Martin County had been formally underway for over three years; the various community forces setting the stage for the utility have been at work considerably longer. This section reviews the obstacles that were overcome and the factors that led to successful implementation of the stormwater utility in Martin County.

Obstacles to Be Overcome

The obstacles that had to be overcome in Martin County were of three types:

1. *Overcoming resistance.* Three major interest groups had to be brought into the project: the engineering community, the environmental community—particularly in the form of the St. Lucie River Initiative, and the residents of the county. These three groups had to agree on an articulation of the problem, that it was of real concern, and that it had to be addressed, even to the point of imposing an additional tax burden on the community. The interplay of these groups set the stage for the board to address the issue.

2. *Devising a legally defensible structure.* Florida constitutional, statutory, and case law are bound together in the creation of the funding device known in Florida as an assessment. While certain generic aspects are clearly defined and even litigated, other aspects of the device are constantly emerging with new case law. Application of the concept to stormwater is relatively recent, so it was critical that it be carefully applied to this new enterprise.

3. *Devising a rate structure perceived to be fair.* Agreement that the stormwater problems facing the community were real and important was only part of the program. Once the community came to consensus concerning the need for action, it had to consent to a specific work program and to a fair basis for funding the program. The utility's rate structure had to assess those parcels that benefited from the services a proportionate share reasonably equal to the amount by which they benefited, and had to exclude from assessment those parcels which did not benefit. The system had to take into account site-specific characteristics that affect the generation of stormwater. And it had to assign reasonably derived credits for those owners who already had reduced their stormwater impact because of investment in private stormwater facilities. It had to address all properties that generated stormwater—residential, commercial, agricultural, and vacant. And it had to distinguish among different basin-level capital programs. Only when a structure was found that could cost effectively handle these issues would the public and the board of county commissioners perceive the system as fair.

The Opportunity for Innovation

Three factors set the stage for innovation in the creation of the utility. First was the nature of the problem itself. The St. Lucie

River system and estuary was increasingly threatened by urbanization and the accumulation of problems quietly piling up over the past decades. A vocal, well-educated constituency was in place, organized and already searching for a way to effect a program to solve the estuary problems.

Second, the county had invested extensively in the creation of a geographic information system (GIS) over the previous five years. The system had matured to the point where physiological and natural systems maps were able to be generated for the first time. These maps were instrumental in the emergent recognition on the part of staff, the steering team, and the citizens committee that stormwater was far more than flood control; that, indeed, it was simply one part of the much larger, more pressing arena of water resource management. The GIS maps allowed the steering team to conceptualize the real problems and to assess their strategic implications.

Third, tropical storm Gordon racked the county with a 50- to 100-year storm event, depending upon what part of the county one was in, coming less than two years after Hurricane Andrew slammed into south Florida. The attendant flood, as well as quality and infrastructure problems associated with Gordon, reminded the community that stormwater could have devastating effects in a very short period of time.

Even if the community was ready to address the stormwater issues, major technical obstacles remained in defining a specific stormwater program and in funding such a program. Innovation in two areas proved as keys to pushing the stormwater program forward.

Shift in Paradigm

For most of the life of the project, the interested parties (staff, environmentalists, engineers, citizens) operated under the standard engineering perception that stormwater was to be engineered to move off land as quickly as possible without causing flooding problems downstream. As discussed previously, only in the latter stages of the project did the perspective emerge that embraced a much larger view of stormwater as part of the management of the limited, critical resource of potable water. The broader perspective led to the incorporation by the steering team of larger-scale solutions that could be integrated with community needs for potable water recharge and backcharge, conservation areas, and passive and active park areas. These large-scale facilities are integrally tied to salinity and contaminant control for the estuary. This approach provides two substantial advantages to the project: a clear platform for reaching the broader community in public information discussions, and a way to bring the engineering community, the water management district, and the environmental community together under the same broad umbrella.

Structural Innovations

The incorporation of several key components into the rate structure facilitated acceptance by the board and the community. These innovations included:

- incorporation of pervious as well as impervious area into the rate model;
- the creation of a credit determination technique, which allowed for differences in site design requirements;
- the use of a two-step apportionment methodology (cost based and parcel based); and
- the tying of benefit to pre-determined levels of service and the elimination of performance deficiencies.

Each solved a specific problem that was perceived by some affected groups as unfair. Each of these techniques was closely tied to a legal tenet designed to provide latent defense of the rate structure.

Important Milestones and Events

Upon reflection, several key events have been noted as milestones in the process of establishing the stormwater utility. They are as follows:

- the board, at a retreat in 1992, articulated stormwater management as one of the top six challenges facing the community. This status was later reconfirmed by the board in a 1995 strategic planning session with staff;

- the three work sessions held with the board where the three reports outlining an emerging program were discussed and approved;

- differences with the engineering community over the county's regulation of and vision for stormwater management were ironed out;

- a cross-discipline team of consultant expertise was retained to facilitate the development of the program and funding mechanisms;

- the board made a commitment to advance funding of critical projects to be reimbursed by the stormwater assessment;

- tropical storm Gordon in August 1994 had a substantial impact on the area;

- a steering team was created composed of senior management staff, local engineers, SFWMD senior staff, and the consultant team; and

- a vision statement was developed that expanded the problem and solution environment to a more encompassing and integrated level.

CONCLUSION AND SUMMARY

The interplay of interest group agenda, real community problems, innovative technical solutions, and fortuitous timing set the stage for success. Several lessons stand out that might be of assistance to other communities struggling with similar challenges:

1. Getting all agencies and players together around the table often leads to a common definition of the problem and a shared vision of the solutions. Both are usually bigger and more encompassing than that constructed by any one player.

2. Complex problems require a multi-discipline team. By integrating engineering and environmental science with law and management systems, all structural hurdles were overcome; single-dimension teams could not have addressed the interwoven aspects necessary to find the solution.

3. Where technical problems are involved, the professional community must endorse the solution before the political actors can embrace it. Endorsement often is a matter of finding a "zone of comfort" within which all members are willing to consent to the approach.

4. The search for solutions must be genuinely open ended. The search will very likely lead in directions other than that originally anticipated; the

team has to be receptive to changes in paradigm to find innovative solutions. Hidden agendas and closed minds will doom the process.

5. Above all, timing is critical; the keys to successful timing are patience, recognizing an open door, and moving forward when the door is opened.

Many hurdles, large and small, remain before the newly-created utility completes the job for which it was created, addressing the water resource management issues facing Martin County. The effort will take decades. But a solid foundation has been laid upon which future efforts can build toward the eventual solution of the stormwater problems of the county.

3

Doing More with Less in Public Safety

CORTEZ LAWRENCE

There are considerable differences of opinion as to what functions are most central to governing. Proponents of various sectors can make persuasive arguments for any one of several activities as the primary function of government, but no segment seems to be more universally accepted as a core function than public safety. At the national, state, and local level, the public safety function has had central prominence in our history—as well as being at the core of issues that the body politic considers most germane to the functioning of government.

This prominence continues today with debates over reallocation of national-level public safety expenditures in the post–Cold War era, the contest over realignments of the states' militia to national defense priorities, the multi-level issues of prisons and justice for perpetrators as well as victims, issues as to life and property safety from natural and man-made disasters, the failure of all efforts to stem the abuse of drugs and the problems attendant to drug abuse, the need to protect the environment and ourselves from hazardous products and processes, current demands for rapid intervention in trauma care, and the increase in violence by youths and gangs.

Demands are high for answers to these problems. According to a 1995 poll published in the March 1995 issue of *PA Times,* public safety issues were listed as the most important items on the agenda for America's cities and towns. National League of Cities President Carolyn Long Banks is quoted in the article:

The concept that emerges from these responses is a belief that I have espoused for many years: namely, that we must shake loose from our conventional thinking about public safety. We need to examine everything that helps to create and maintain safe, secure homes, neighborhoods and cities.

The public safety sector of government consumes a large share of budget expenditures for most local governments. A review of recent budgets shows a trend of about one-third of a local government's non-utility expenditures are targeted for public safety. The "raison de vie" for local government existence historically centers on enforcement of the government's police powers. The amount of resources generally devoted to public safety illuminates the need for innovations in service delivery.

Staffing costs are the largest single element in the budget of most public safety organizations. It is common for personnel costs, including benefits, to consume in excess of 90 percent of a fire or police department's non-capital budget. This ratio reflects the labor-intensive nature of the work. Combating and preventing fires and crimes require a sufficient number of trained personnel. Salaries in the public safety services have to be adequate to attract capable people. Additional costs may be generated by Fair Labor Standards Act impositions, higher insurance costs to offset the job risks, aging of the work force, pay inflation, and other indirect costs.

To counter high personnel costs, some cities and towns choose to provide their fire protection through the use of volunteers. Many volunteer systems have enviable records of service and, in fact, provide a vast majority of the organized fire protection within the United States. A community considers several factors in choosing between volunteer or paid fire services. Among these are labor relations, response time requirements, availability of volunteer population, hazard analysis, community traditions, and economic demands. Communities have also used volunteers to supplement career police staffing. Rarely are police volunteers the sole source of personnel in any public safety organization. There are many reported successes with auxiliary and reserve programs nationwide.

Volunteers, however, entail considerable "hidden costs" and most certainly are not free. They may prove difficult to recruit, require training, turnover frequently, need special leadership, utilize resources, and generate unique internal and external issues for organizations. Overall, volunteers remain a viable option for communities for a variety of services under appropriate circumstances, and represent an obvious potential for savings of a portion of staffing costs.

Another option that local governments have utilized to reduce the high cost of personnel is to consolidate service delivery with other units of government. There are numerous examples of consolidation of public safety services, such as single communication centers that serve several cities and counties within a geographical area. Another example is the elimination by smaller cities of their jails made possible through the contracting for that service with an adjoining jurisdiction. Phenix City, Alabama, was able to close its city jail when Russell County enlarged its jail and contracted to provide that service to Phenix City.

Auburn, Alabama, a city of approximately 40,000 residents in the eastern part of the state, is best known as the home of the state's largest university, Auburn University. Like many university cities, Auburn has experienced growth in industrial, commercial, and residential sectors over the past two decades. This growth has created pressure on the city government to be innovative in the delivery of services. Since public safety consumes nearly 35 percent of the city's general fund budget, the city has examined carefully more efficient ways of providing quality public safety services.

The case study that follows describes two of the innovative solutions that Auburn developed to provide quality public safety services at substantial cost savings. In the first, the city government took advantage of a number of factors in the community to develop an entirely new approach to providing trained firefighters while giving college students the opportunity to finance their educations. In the second, an apparent duplication of service with the local hospital convinced the city manager and the hospital administrator that consolidation was a better approach to delivering emergency medical services.

AUBURN'S STUDENT FIREFIGHTER PROGRAM

Due to community growth, Auburn was facing a need to increase staffing for fire service operations in the spring of 1989 but had only limited resources to allocate for new personnel. In considering the available options, the city's management dismissed the option of using volunteer firefighters because of the need for additional on-duty firefighters. There was not enough money available to increase staffing to desired levels with regular, career firefighters.

The city manager directed the Public Safety Department staff to investigate the possibility of developing a supplemental, full-time firefighter work force from the student body from nearby Auburn University. The city manager's concept was that these "student firefighters" would be basic level firefighters who were also full-time students. They would be trained to the state-mandated level, paid for their work hours as temporary, full-time employees who would leave the program upon graduation.

This was not a totally new concept for the city manager. He was exposed years earlier to a similar concept while a student at the University of Maryland, where students who served as volunteer firefighters were provided living quarters in the station as payment in kind. Other institutions provide various arrangements for students involved in firefighting, but all center on the concept of students providing manpower to the sponsoring entity.

Auburn's program, while not completely original or unique, is an amalgam of various programs and concepts borrowed from around the country. In 1989, the city manager and public safety director developed an outline for a student program that included pay at minimum wage for the student firefighters, provisions for in-station living, and student company autonomy (i.e., separate companies operated and led by student members). On this basis, the staff began planning the implementation of such a program. The initial plan was to provide a program for full-time college students (defined as those taking 10 or more quarter hours credit attempted in at least three of four academic quarters of the year, with appropriate adjustments for semester equivalents), to allow living in the fire station, and to pay a wage that provided enough money to attend school and to meet basic living expense needs. The city manager presented his plan to the city council in 1989.

After being convinced that the staff had done a thorough job in evaluating the proposed program, the city council unanimously endorsed it and included funding in the budget for its implementation.

During the spring and early summer, the staff recruited students from Auburn University, Tuskegee University, and the local community college for the initial group of student firefighters. The response from the students was strong enough to allow the staff to choose from many applicants. After thorough screening, the first group of recruits was hired to begin the fall quarter in 1989.

The next challenge to implementation of the program was a provision of Alabama law that requires paid firefighters to meet the career firefighter minimum training standards. The law specifically proscribes in-service training; therefore, the city staff had to conduct a full recruit school for six weeks in August/September 1989 before assigning the students to duty.

Because there was no firefighting experience in the student group, leaders for the student firefighters had to be recruited and trained. City management thought this might be a problem, since many of the career firefighters apparently were opposed to the program. Many career personnel indicated that they viewed it as a threat to job security and as a way the city might avoid creation of new career firefighter positions. Some of the firefighters had been in litigation against the city. In settlement of that litigation, the city agreed to establish a personnel floor in the fire division through 1997, which somewhat ameliorated the concerns about job security. The federal judge's order in the settlement also made it obvious that the city had the right to maintain its student program and could consider exclusive use of student firefighters in future fire stations.

Prior to the initial recruit school in 1989, five career firefighters volunteered to serve as program leaders and were trained as team leaders. Two were paramedics; three were line firefighters, one of whom also served as a chief of a volunteer department in the county. The initial team leaders averaged seven years' career service, with the least experienced having served less than three years and the most experienced having over 12 years of service. All five team leaders, who were paid at the lieutenant's rate of pay, had various amounts of college credit and were actively enrolled in correspondence or resident courses at the time of selection. Since then, one has completed course work for his Ph.D., and the others have graduated with their baccalaureate degrees.

The program started immediately after recruit school ended in September 1989. The students were divided into four teams, with the initial shift assignment being four days of 12-hour shifts on duty followed by four days off duty. The practice included changing shifts at noon and midnight so that members could schedule morning or evening classes. Initially, the students were used to staff a manpower squad but this changed in the winter of 1990. As students became proficient at pump operations through in-service and specialized training, they were assigned to staff the pumper at their station.

In 1991, the students were placed on the same 24-hour shift as the career firefighters and have remained on that shift since that time. Those with a class scheduled during work hours are excused from duty to attend class but must return to work if called or as soon as classes are over. While this arrangement has proven popular with the students, it does place a burden on the team leader if several students' classes and work schedules conflict. It requires careful planning on the team leader's part to ensure he has adequate staffing at any specific time.

The program has evolved through practice. For example, in the planning phase, the city staff did not envision various pay steps for the student firefighters. In fact, several pay steps have been instituted. Starting recruits get slightly more than the minimum wage. Five-percent step increases follow when they are certified as firefighter I (the state minimum level)—with another step increase for qualifying as a driver and a last step for certification as a firefighter II. These increases are coupled with time-in-service requirements.

The living quarters provided have not proven to be popular with the students. The student fire station is typical in that it has a large common dorm room and day room for firefighters. Ideally, a station would have semi-private rooms that would provide more privacy for studying. Semi-private rooms would increase the likelihood of students living in the station, which would increase response numbers substantially.

Challenges Faced

According to their superiors and to observers, the students have proven to be outstanding firefighters and pump operators. They bring energy, talent, drive, and, in some cases, even some specialized knowledge to the fire division. However, like many innovations, implementation of the program has not been without trials.

The student firefighters were called "baby firemen" and other terms denigrating their ability as firefighters, mostly by the career fire staff during a period of initial animosity. The nature of the program is that the students will never accumulate much experience. Therefore, performance standards are achieved through tough, demanding, high-quality training. Setting high standards, training the candidates to them, and evaluating how closely they come to meeting them are integral parts of the program's success. After seven years, the result has been the full acceptance and integration of career and student companies in operations.

The team leaders are a critical element in the program. The initial five team leaders withstood the disapproval of many of their peers when they took the positions. Part of their recompense has been to continue their education and training, preparing them for future assignments in fire service leadership positions. The position of team leader is often more challenging than those of their colleagues who serve as company officers in career companies. The student firefighter program offers team leaders unique opportunities for growth. Interestingly, three of the four top finishers in an assessment process for fire captain were team leaders, as is the current fire chief.

Financial Benefits of the Program

The cost-effectiveness of the student firefighter program is obvious. If the city were to staff every student slot with a career firefighter, it would spend at least three times as much on salary and benefits. In the future, additional required firefighters will be students. The city plans to build two additional fire stations over the next decade and both are to be staffed with students.

In comparing costs between student and career staffing, the city assumes the staffing will be three student firefighters and one team leader versus three career firefighters and one lieutenant. The cost of pay and benefits for the team leader and lieutenant are equal, so there is no advantage in either option. Using a factor of firefighters of 3.4 to assure constant manning of each position on a 24/48-hour staffing basis, the city would need 10.2 firefighters to provide the necessary manpower. In Auburn, the average firefighter hourly rate is $10 an hour plus $2 in benefit costs. When the total hourly cost, $12 an hour, is multiplied by the annual work hours per firefighter (2,920) times 10.2, the cost to the city is $357,408. By comparison, the student firefighters staff the new station at $5.15 an hour plus $0.25 in benefits per student firefighter. Using the same formula as above, the results are $5.15 × 2,920 × 10.2 = $153,388. The student program is less than one-half the cost of career staffing, with an annual net savings of $204,020. The savings would allow Auburn to staff an additional fire station with career team leaders and a student firefighter company for the same expenditure. It is likely that cities in other regions will experience even greater savings per firefighter, since Auburn and the entire Southeast tend to be on the lower end of firefighter pay scales.

Conclusion

Auburn's student firefighter program is a viable alternative to providing quick-response fire services at a fraction of the costs associated with career personnel. Another, unintended benefit has been that the most recent career hires have been former student firefighters. The student firefighters have to compete for all career positions with those in the general applicant pool. They are given no advantage because of their participation in the student firefighter program. However, the student firefighters have consistently outperformed other applicants on entrance tests.

The issues identified and addressed by the city's management are the following:

1. Enhancement of working conditions. The city could not afford additional career firefighters, and, in fact, had used paid, on-call volunteers to supplement staffing at high-demand fires in the past. The student firefighters provide instant, on-scene, professionally trained, and professionally led firefighters who assist the career force in firefighting. Spreading the workload through the addition of student firefighters has obvious benefits to all on-scene workers, as more hands are available to do any given task.

2. *No threat to job security for existing workers.* In a court settlement not directly related to these issues, the city committed itself to maintenance of a career firefighter staffing of a specific minimum until 1997. Additionally, the city manager committed that downsizing of the career force would be done only through attrition. This has proven to be the case in practice and all parties are apparently satisfied.

3. *Position security.* While the city retains the right and obligation to review, modify, and even eliminate jobs as needed, management has recognized the need for a core of competent professionals to staff the essential functions of the fire organization, as well as to provide team leadership for the student firefighters. The growth of the community requires career firefighter personnel to maintain the administrative, technical, and leadership functions of the fire service. With additional growth, the city may need to have additional career positions to handle these functions and support the student firefighter program.

Today, the Auburn student firefighter program continues to provide a firefighting force of energetic, motivated, and enthusiastic workers who do not impose long-term burdens on personnel costs while providing its members an opportunity to fund an education at a major university, to learn a profession, to participate in government at the "street level bureaucrat" level, and to graduate with considerable work experience. Graduates of the student firefighter program have demonstrated an excellent grasp of teamwork, an understanding of organizational behavior, and considerable self-confidence in having participated in an overtly dangerous and physically demanding activity.

CONSOLIDATION OF EMERGENCY MEDICAL SERVICES

In early July 1989, several fire units responded to an accident resulting in several injuries in Auburn. These units were closely followed by an ambulance provided by the county-chartered hospital. Firefighters trained as paramedics conducted triage of the patients, mitigated injuries, and packaged patients for transport.

At that point, the patients were handed over to the hospital transport service for transportation to the nearby emergency room. This model for two levels of providers in emergency medical service (EMS) delivery was common on television shows, such as "Emergency" in the 1970s, and is in use in many areas today.

After July 1989, the service providers in the above scenario changed. Now hospital units positioned in Auburn respond directly to calls for assistance and carry along sufficient resources to perform most EMS calls unaided. In a contractual arrangement with East Alabama Medical Center (EAMC), the city divested itself of operating an EMS and rescue service by consolidating its service with the ambulance service provided by the hospital. The contract requires EAMC to provide an ambulance staffed with two paramedics and a second ambulance staffed by two additional paramedics who also "cross-man" a rescue truck full-time.

Background and History

In 1981, the cities of Auburn and Opelika, Lee County, and the EAMC governing board reached an agreement concerning the provision and production of EMS services in Lee County. Under that agreement, EAMC produced transportation services county-wide, while each of the cities provided and produced emergency medical intervention and rescue services within the city and its respective end of the county. In addition, each government unit subsidized the equipping and staffing of EAMC's ambulance during non-business hours. One medic and one driver staffed the EAMC operation during business hours. Staffing was by a single driver/ paramedic after hours, with the cities providing for an additional paramedic from their own resources after hours to reduce the cost to the hospital's system. During business hours, EAMC furnished two-person staffing to meet needs. Because of Auburn's more distant location from the hospital, the transport unit was co-located at the Auburn fire division main station after hours. During the day, the ambulances were located at the hospital, five miles from the station.

The Opportunity

In 1987, the city manager appointed a director of public safety and gave him responsibility for managing the city's police and fire services, code enforcement, and the 911 communications center. Several changes took place in terms of personnel and structure around the time of the creation of the public safety department. Both the police and fire chiefs departed in 1987; responsibility for code enforcement was focused into one division, and police and fire communications were consolidated within the department.

With the new department of public safety in place, the city manager asked the new director to study the feasibility of consolidating the city's EMS function that was housed in the fire division with the hospital's ambulance service. After considerable study, the city manager and the public safety director agreed that the city could save in excess of $100,000 per year through consolidation. They decided to call for a meeting with the hospital administrator to discuss their findings and determine whether the hospital had any interest in consolidation.

At the meeting, the city manager and the public safety director presented the details of the idea to the hospital administrator. They were pleased with the positive response of the administrator, who informed them of an experience he had had only the week before. The hospital administrator had observed an automobile accident at the local mall. The response included a paramedic/rescue truck, a fire pumper, the fire shift commander's vehicle, an ambulance, and more than one police car. All these units had responded in emergency mode—driving through intersections, against traffic signals, and at high speed. The accident turned out to be inconsequential, with no persons being treated or transported. The administrator related this event to the city manager, along with his own concerns over duplication of effort and services and the sheer number of units that responded to this call. They agreed that the public was not well served economically by the duplication of services and was even ill served by the exacerbation of highway risks associated with emergency responses.

Analysis and Solution

In the analysis of Auburn's EMS program, the city manager and the public safety director considered response requirements, nature of calls, resources actually needed on scene, staffing, and the cost of operating the current system. The results were that the quality of service was generally good, but with important exceptions based

on physician complaints concerning some procedures and personnel. The budget cost of the EMS operation was $331,000 for 1989.
This figure did not include the $36,000 supplement paid to the
EAMC for ambulance subsidy, nor any indirect costs that were not
singularly attributable to the EMS operation. The city manager
was only interested in including in the analysis those costs that
would "go away" with the divestment of the EMS service. He
could have prorated administrative overhead in calculations of the
savings generated by EMS divestment, but chose not to do so since
those costs, in general, would continue. For instance, he could have
allocated a portion of the secretarial time to the savings from EMS
divestment, but in reality neither the job nor person was going
away, nor would they become available for general assignment
outside the fire division.

The city leadership identified many places throughout the nation
that provide EMS/rescue service through another government
agency, consolidated agencies, or contract with private providers.
The public safety director made visits to several cities that had
single providers for EMS and ambulance service. While the production model most often observed was private, some models allowed both government provision and production or any
combination of public and private mixes. The private delivery operations observed were well run, enjoyed a good reputation, had
professional staffing, enjoyed a high collection rate and, in general,
seemed effective at minimal cost to the local government. This type
of system had the potential to maintain quality of patient care and
remove the inefficiencies of the multiple response system.

In a June 1989 memorandum to the city council members, the
city manager emphasized the economic issues that would be most
persuasive in the council's consideration of contracting for rescue
and ambulance services with EAMC. The fiscal year (FY) 1990 cost
of city operation of the EMS at $352,000 versus the hospital's
proposal of $219,000 was the focal point for council considera-
tion. The city manager also discussed response times, availability
of units, equipment, and personnel issues. In the proposed contract
with EAMC, the city's paramedics would be offered positions with
the EAMC paramedic service at the same pay and similar benefits,
and with continuation of their Retirement Systems of Alabama accounts. The paramedics who chose to accept employment with

EAMC were offered the option of returning to city employment within a year without diminution of pay. They were also given the option of staying with the city as firefighters without a reduction in pay, including the extra pay for paramedic certification.

Evaluation

In June 1989, the Auburn city council voted to approve the contract for consolidating the city's EMS with the hospital's ambulance service. Fire division personnel attempted to generate some public support against the consolidation. They sought forums to generate public interest in the issue. However, very little controversy was generated among the public, and the measure was passed by the city council, with implementation scheduled for July.

Today, the joint agreement continues, with ambulance/EMS services provided by EAMC to the citizens of Auburn. The consolidation of services has gone smoothly with strong citizen support. Three primary benefits have accrued to the community as a result of consolidation. First, the city has saved well over $1 million during the first seven years of the contract. Second, since two ambulances are now kept in the city 24 hours per day, the response time for ambulance transport has diminished and patients have gotten to the hospital faster. Third, liability for the city has decreased because it no longer directly produces a service that has numerous risk factors that may lead to litigation.

All citizens receive the economic benefits that are generated by the contracting-out decision. The increase in contract costs to the city has been modest—$263,050 for FY 1996, up $44,050 from the $219,000 of 1989. The FY 1996 number includes money paid by the city for the annual purchase of replacement ambulance units instead of funding separate EAMC requests for new ambulances as needed as was the practice in FY 1990. There are no increases in costs to the patient that would not have been experienced under the old system. Prior to consolidation, patients were charged for transport and supplies used by both the hospital and fire paramedics. They received no fire division bill, as the fire paramedics would replenish their supplies from the hospital unit, then the hospital would do the billing for the supplies used by the city's EMS. Under the contract, patients who are not transported are not billed.

What has this meant for the EAMC? There are several advantages to a consolidated EMS/rescue operation, according to the EAMC administrator. He sees one role of the hospital in the community that of being a "good citizen." EAMC has a responsibility to help local governments meet their needs, whenever possible. In the medical field, he believes the hospital can provide higher-quality services to the community, reduce service duplication, and allow local governments to specialize in those services that they do best and most efficiently. He admits there are several advantages to the hospital's providing the ambulance service to a community. In this period of competition for patients, the hospital's ability to control the ambulance service allows it to fill hospital beds from patients brought to it by ambulance.

The city has realized constant savings in direct operating costs. The hospital collects most of its billables and receives a supplement from each governmental agency in Lee County. There has been no published analysis of the costs to citizens, but informal studies have indicated that there are no significant differences, once adjusted for mileage, between the costs of an Auburn citizen being injured and requiring a trip to EAMC via ambulance and the same accident happening in nearby cities. Cities that have maintained dual systems probably cost the citizen more since they are paying twice for paramedic service, once through the city's general fund and once through ambulance billing.

Conclusion

These two innovations by Auburn public administrators have saved the city several million dollars during the seven years since their implementation. Both were met initially with opposition from within the fire division but had strong support from elected officials and citizens. In both cases, the city manager and the public safety director investigated the feasibility of the innovation with the knowledge that funds were limited for expansion of fire and EMS services. They realized that if the level of service needed for the community was to be provided, better ways of producing both services had to be found. They were successful in building support from within the organization, in the community, and among other agencies, such as the hospital and the university. The city of Auburn has now institutionalized both innovations, and it is likely that both will be part of the way the city provides public safety services for many years.

4

Organizing against Losses

STEVEN A. REEVES

Risk management is concerned with the protection of organizational assets from the adverse effects of accidental losses. By protecting against these losses, risk management enhances the use of resources for productive purposes and the accomplishment of organizational objectives. The practice of risk management uses a variety of techniques to reduce the occurrence of losses, to reduce the severity of losses when they occur, and to prepare for the financial consequences of losses so that an organization can continue to operate and accomplish its mission. In an era of fiscal constraints and demands for more, and higher quality, service, risk management has become one of the most important and exciting management opportunities in local government.

Early municipal risk management efforts emphasized financial transfers of risk through the purchase of commercial insurance. When losses did occur, insurance absorbed the financial impact. This was an effective risk management strategy because commercial insurance coverage was available and affordable. However, this practice came to a crashing halt for many entities in the mid-1980s when liability insurance premiums skyrocketed and coverage became restricted. Many observers have blamed this "insurance crisis" on expanding municipal tort liability throughout the United

States, and on the poor underwriting practices of the insurance industry during the late 1970s and early 1980s.

During this period, many states saw the demise of "sovereign immunity," and local governments began to experience added liability exposure through legal concepts such as comparative negligence and the interpretation of laws such as Section 1983, United States Code, Title 42. Although liability risks were growing, the insurance industry, rather than basing premiums upon expected losses, was lured by the high interest rates of the era to sell its products at artificially low prices in order to increase available investment dollars. As interest rates declined and losses mounted, the insurance industry responded with higher premiums and reduced coverages. A National League of Cities issue paper pointed out in 1986:

> Cancellations of liability insurance policies and astronomical increases in premiums (sometimes more than 1,000 percent) are creating a growing crisis for local governments. While the liability insurance crisis affects individual professionals and businesses as well as local government, cities have been particularly and disproportionately affected. The average increase in the cost of premiums for cities able to obtain liability insurance in 1985 was 650 percent.
>
> Because of the diversity and the complexity of government activities and responsibilities, local governments are exposed to many types of risk. The massive de facto withdrawal of insurance companies from the municipal market and skyrocketing premiums have created a major financial crisis for cities throughout the nation. But more than public funds are at risk. In many cases the very capacity of cities to serve the public is seriously impaired; some services have been terminated because insurance coverage has either been drastically reduced or simply not available. The ultimate cost is borne by the taxpayers and citizens of each affected community.

One community that was caught up in this insurance crisis, and benefited from the innovation catalyst that the crisis provided, was Tallahassee, Florida.

TALLAHASSEE, FLORIDA

The city of Tallahassee, Florida, is located on wooded rolling hills in the "Big Bend" area of the Gulf Coast. This beautiful 170-

year-old city is the state capital and home to Florida State University. The city of Tallahassee is a full-service government, including water, gas, and electric utilities, public transportation, and an airport. It provides services to approximately 130,000 residents within its 80 square miles of incorporated area. Tallahassee experienced tremendous growth in the 1980s. The population, consisting of relatively young and well-educated residents, increased by 53 percent while the incorporated land area grew by over 126 percent. Commercial and residential development activity paralleled the growth in the population and land area of Tallahassee. Although government is the mainstay of the local economy, economic diversification is occurring.

Tallahassee utilizes a commission-manager form of government. The five-member commission appoints the city manager, the treasurer clerk, the city attorney, and the city auditor. All city departments are under the organizational authority of the city manager, except the departments headed by the other appointed officials. The risk management program is a function of the treasurer clerk's department. Today, the city employs more than 2,800 people. In the mid-1980s, approximately 2,000 people were employed by Tallahassee city government.

The Insurance Advisory Board

One unique unit of the city government is a citizens' group called the Insurance Advisory Board. In 1955, the City of Tallahassee created the Insurance Advisory Board to advise the city commission on insurance needs and to provide assistance to the city in its insurance procurement efforts. The five members of this board are appointed by the city commission from among nominees submitted by local commercial insurance agents. Nominees must be local insurance agents who possess certain expertise in the area of commercial insurance. The board is charged with reviewing the city's insurance requirements, preparing the specifications in requests for proposals for insurance coverages, analyzing and evaluating insurance proposals, and making recommendations to the city commission in regard to insurance carriers and coverage. The board works very closely with the risk management division and, in a real sense, is an advocate to that division's efforts. Meetings of the board occur on a quarterly basis and are attended by risk management personnel, the treasurer clerk, and the city attorney.

According to John E. Hunt, Jr., a former member the board who served during the mid-1980s, the members of the board were well-respected members of the community and enjoyed a good relationship with the city commission. He believes that the city commission respected the advice of the board on insurance matters.

THE INSURANCE CRISIS HITS TALLAHASSEE

Like many cities throughout the United States, Tallahassee relied heavily on commercial insurance to protect against the costs of liability claims, accidents, and other unexpected losses. Two very large loss exposure areas, general and auto liability, were insured through the Home Insurance Company. Typical general liability exposures for municipalities include injuries and damages associated with sidewalk defects, road hazards, sign maintenance, sewage backups, service interruptions, and parks and recreation facilities and programs. Auto liability arises from injuries and damages associated with the negligent operation of vehicles. Both types of exposure are generally related to the negligent, careless, or unskillful performance of duties.

Tallahassee's insurance premiums for the general and auto liability exposures had been gradually increasing during FY1980–1985. Then, in mid-1984, without warning, the Home Insurance Company notified the city that in 30 days both the city's general and auto liability insurance policies would be canceled, despite the fact that total losses, including reserves, had been running well below average premiums of $400,000 per year.

The immediate problem for the City of Tallahassee was to find replacement insurance coverage for general and auto liability. The immediate solution came from the Florida League of Cities, which operated a liability insurance pool program for Florida's cities. Insurance coverage was provided through the league between 1984 and September 1986. However, insurance premiums continued to increase, and by fiscal year 1986 total general and auto liability premiums had grown to $921,000. In addition, the league anticipated a 30 percent increase in premiums, for a total of $1.2 million in FY 1987. It was during this period that the city began considering self-insurance of the general and auto liability exposures it faced.

Following the cancellation of the insurance coverage, and during the league's coverage period, the insurance advisory board began discussing with the city's long-time insurance officer, the treasurer clerk, and the city attorney the idea of self-insuring the city's general and auto liability exposures. These city officials expressed support for the self-insurance concept and its possible application to general and auto liability exposures. They concluded that some perceived advantages of self-insuring these exposures included lower overall costs, better claims service, more latitude in deciding which claims to settle or defend, and a greater loss control incentive for the city. Following these discussions, and as part of its insurance renewal recommendation for FY 1986, the insurance advisory board recommended to the city commission that the city study its loss history with a view toward the feasibility of self-insuring its general and auto liability exposures beginning in FY 1987.

HIRING A RISK MANAGER

As mentioned earlier, many cities' risk management efforts relied heavily upon risk transfer through the purchase of commercial insurance. This was true of the city of Tallahassee, and although a safety program existed to minimize accidents and injuries, the broader loss or liability exposures were generally handled through the financial protection afforded by insurance. For many years, Tallahassee employed an insurance officer to manage the city's insurance program. The focus of this position was the acquisition of insurance and claims processing activities, and not other facets of risk management such as loss avoidance and reduction. As discussions were beginning on self-insurance, the city's insurance officer suddenly died, leaving a position vacancy.

Rather than filling the position of insurance officer, the city decided that it was time to move into a more broadly focused risk management program, a program that incorporated a greater emphasis on loss exposure identification, analysis, and control in all loss exposure areas. Consequently, the city began recruitment efforts to attract a qualified risk manager who would be able to manage a broad-based self-insured program.

Tallahassee's early recruitment efforts attracted the interest of Jimmy Glisson, the risk manager for the city of Gainesville, Florida. Glisson's experience included the development and management of self-insured workers compensation, and auto liability and general liability programs for the city of Gainesville. However, Glisson did not initially apply for the job because the advertised salary was not competitive, but he did provide some early assistance to Tallahassee in defining what a risk management program should include, how to develop and manage self-insured programs, and the skills and abilities needed to lead successfully a risk management effort. As the difficulty of recruiting a qualified risk manager at the advertised salary became apparent, the insurance advisory board explained the need for a higher salary to the city commission in order for the city to fill the position. With an increase in the salary authorized by the commission, the recruitment effort moved forward. Ultimately, with applicant screening assistance provided by the advisory board, Jimmy Glisson was hired in February 1986.

Problems with the League's Insurance Program

For many years, the city had enjoyed a positive relationship with the Florida League of Cities, located just across the street from city hall. Members of the city staff had been very active and assumed leadership roles in league activities, programs, and associations. And it was the league of cities that stepped in and provided insurance when the city's insurance was canceled in 1984. Nevertheless, even with the league's program, the problem of high insurance premiums compared to losses remained an issue for the city. An additional problem arose due to poor claims service by the league's program, largely the result of not being able to reach the adjustor when a claim incident had occurred. As expressed by the city attorney, the league program was a good interim solution but it simply was not a permanent solution for Tallahassee.

Preparing the Self-Insurance Program

The insurance advisory board had done early groundwork for developing a self-insured general and auto liability program by recommending a self-insurance feasibility study. The existing acceptance and support by the treasurer clerk and the city attorney of the self-insurance concept as applied to Tallahassee's general and auto liability exposures was also an important element upon which Glisson was able to build a risk management program.

Glisson's first task was to study the city's five-year loss history, determine if losses were predictable enough on an annual basis to assume the significant financial risk of self-insurance, compare losses against paid premiums, and determine if it would be economically feasible to enter into a self-insured auto and general liability program. Glisson did this during February and early March 1986 and produced a report to the insurance advisory board advocating the self-insurance initiative. The board unanimously voted to accept the report and to recommend to the city commission that the auto and general liability self-insured programs be initiated as part of the 1987 fiscal year budget.

With the "mandate" from the advisory board, the risk manager, treasurer clerk, and city attorney began preparing a self-insurance program proposal for submission to the commission. Major considerations included self-insurance funding, excess or stop loss insurance, claims handling, legal support, and loss prevention. Based on the analysis of loss history, the proposal recommended that the city budget $600,000 in the self-insurance fund for payment of claims and claims handling services during FY 1987. This amount would be backed by a $3 million insurance reserve fund already in existence, and finally by the city's deficiency and emergency fund, which contained an estimated $8–10 million.

In the proposal, Glisson recommended that claims handling, which entails investigating claims, determining liability and legitimate claim value, and claims settlement, be contracted out to a professional claims adjusting service. Among the recognized advantages of contracting for claims handling is the promotion of an unbiased claims adjusting reputation that helps to depoliticize potentially volatile events by enabling city officials to "accept" the recommendations of a professional third party, rather than having to make decisions within a political context. On the other hand, because the city acts as the insurer, and ultimately controls settlement decisions, it can override the recommendations of the adjustor. This is especially helpful when a claim has become politically charged or when the city simply feels that a settlement is not in the best interest of the city. Other advantages of "outsourcing" these services include 24-hour claims service without directly bearing costs associated with staff employment and associated risks (e.g., workers compensation losses, health care costs, employment-related litigation). Because the city would be a party to the claims service contract, it would have contractual control over performance problems and would be able to deal directly with those problems instead of going through another entity, as the city did with the league's program.

Support for the auto and general liability self-insurance program would be provided by the city attorney. This was viewed as a very positive element of being self-insured because the attorney would be directly involved in litigation decisions—rather than these decisions being made between an insurer and its appointed lawyer.

A final element of the proposed program was to establish a loss prevention program within risk management that went beyond employee safety issues. This would be accomplished through the employment of a loss control specialist whose efforts would be devoted to the identification and treatment of loss exposures and the provision of support to the self-insurance program. In its actual implementation, the risk management program incorporated a "cost allocation" mechanism so that each department became financially accountable for losses based upon loss experience. This provided an inducement for departments to partner with risk management in the loss control area.

Summarizing the benefits of a self-insurance program in the proposal, the risk manager stated:

A sound risk retention program (self-insurance) has numerous benefits, the most pronounced being (1) it eliminates the cost of risk transfer, (2) the city gains control over claims administration, (3) it focuses attention on loss control and prevention rather than loss paying, (4) greatly improved public relations with the citizens, and (5) gives the city, rather than an insurance company, complete control over and use of all savings realized and reserves being held for open files.

Location of the Risk Management Function

To this point, the city's insurance program had been administered through the treasurer clerk and the safety program had been administered through the city manager's office. The proposed risk management program envisioned the incorporation of these two functions under one unit and, as the scope of the new risk management program became apparent, the city manager argued that the program should be under his operational supervision. The treasurer clerk and the insurance advisory board disagreed. While it was recognized that in most organizations, the risk management program would be under the control of the city manager, those that disagreed felt that it should remain under the authority of treasurer clerk due to the financial responsibilities of that job. Also, by locating the function of risk management under the treasurer clerk, the risk manager would be able to deal with department heads outside their chain of command, and would not be "squeezed" through their contacts or influence with the city manager. Finally, the insurance function had been located with the treasurer clerk for 20 years, an arrangement that the city commission liked. In order to resolve this disagreement, several meetings were held, culminating in a meeting attended by the city manager, treasurer clerk, safety officer, risk manager, and the members of the insurance advisory board. After discussing the issues, the advisory board members stated that they would recommend to the commission, if asked, that the new risk management program be under the control of the treasurer clerk. The city manager ultimately accepted the proposed arrangement; however, it was agreed that the safety function would remain within his chain of command. The city manager made clear his commitment to funding the safety program at a level necessary to ensure its success as an element of the total risk management effort.

With the turf issue resolved, the city administration was able to move forward as a unified group supporting the self-insurance program.

The Presentation

In April 1986, the proposal to adopt the self-insurance program was placed on the city commission agenda by the treasurer clerk and the insurance advisory board. The agenda item request was accompanied by a written report summarizing the background of the request, the feasibility and risks of self-insurance, the proposed structure and implementation of the self-insurance program, and the substantial cost savings anticipated. The report stated that in FY 1987, the city could expect a $170,000 liability cost reduction, with additional savings in future years. In addition, had the city been self-insured during the previous five years, it would have had savings of approximately $175,000 per year. Finally, the report noted that the cost to fund the program would only be $600,000 as compared to an anticipated $1.2 million if the city stayed with the league program.

At the conclusion of their presentation, a member of the insurance advisory board expressed the board's strong endorsement of the proposal and announced that the city manager was in agreement with the proposed structure and would support the program. With very little discussion, the proposed program was unanimously approved by the city commission.

IN RETROSPECT

City officials praise the success of the risk management program. They estimate that millions of dollars have been saved by not purchasing commercial liability insurance. These savings have resulted from avoiding the risk transfer cost (i.e., the premium amount exceeding expected losses), the investment interest that the city earns on the money that would have been paid to the insurance company, and better management of the city's risk exposures. One city report estimates a $500,000 annual savings in the general liability area alone.

Other identified benefits to the city include a heightened awareness of loss exposures and how to manage those exposures, a focus on loss control rather than loss payment, a reduction in loss experience, more effective use of tax dollars, better claims administration, greater control over litigation and other legal matters, greater citizen satisfaction with the city government, and a reduced risk environment that makes Tallahassee a safer place in which to live. In sum, the city's decision to initiate a risk management program provided three valuable benefits: significant financial savings, better management, and improved citizen service and satisfaction.

FROM CRISIS TO SUCCESS

The loss of the financial security provided by insurance can be debilitating to the operation and service delivery of local government. Almost equally problematic can be the dramatic escalation of costs in one area at the expense of other demands. During the mid-1980s, the city of Tallahassee experienced both of these problems as a result of a crisis situation in the commercial liability insurance market. And yet, through crisis, the city was led to innovate within its own structure and operations by establishing a risk management program that incorporated self-insurance of certain loss exposures. By all accounts, Tallahassee's risk management program has been successful.

One theme of this book is that crisis is a fertile breeding ground for innovation and that it creates a willingness to explore and adopt non-traditional solutions. Escalating insurance premiums and the cancellation of insurance coverage created an environment in which city officials agreed not only that something needed to be done to provide financial security against unexpected losses but also that a non-traditional approach was worthy of consideration. This environment was significant to the successful development and implementation of the program in that it created what some city officials described as a supportive and cooperative spirit among the highest-ranking officials.

The financial savings that were anticipated through self-insurance and the establishment of the risk management program were obviously critical to the decision to move forward. Had the numbers not revealed potential significant savings, the willingness to accept the financial risk of self-insurance would have been lacking. Perhaps of greater importance, however, was the support from top management (the treasurer clerk, city manager, and city attorney) and the insurance advisory board, all appointees of the city commission. Had there not been consensus among these individuals to support the program, it is less likely that the commission would have been willing to implement a self-insurance program. The fact that consensus was achieved prior to meeting with the commission is also an important factor in determining why the program was adopted and implemented and why it was successful.

The only opposition to the implementation of the program came from the Florida League of Municipalities, probably because it stood to lose its second largest account. However, the league did not mount a concerted effort to block implementation of the program. Interestingly, the media either did not pick up on the story or treated the development of the program as a non-event. Consequently, there was not a media spotlight on or media debate about the advantages or disadvantages of the self-insurance program.

Central to the success of the program was the quality of the staff charged with its development and implementation. Several city officials noted that staff skills in the areas of finance and public relations contributed to the ultimate success of the program. The city commission respected, and had confidence in, the insurance advisory board and the management staff and acted upon their recommendations. The risk manager played a key leadership role in selling and building the program and was not perceived as a threat by the city's department heads. Cost allocation to fund the self-insurance program created an incentive for department heads to support risk management and utilize the services available through the risk manager.

Financial savings, support, and consensus among top decision-makers, staff ability and leadership, and minimal opposition were important factors contributing to the successful development and implementation of Tallahassee's risk management program. However, without the crisis in the insurance market serving as a change catalyst, the city may not have realized the benefits it now enjoys through its risk management program.

5

From Prescriptive to Performance Zoning

ROBERT J. JUSTER

Throughout the twentieth century, municipal policymakers have increasingly sought ways to influence the use of land within their corporate boundaries. During the past 70 years, their search has led to the creation of a system of regulatory devices through which change in the urban environment can be influenced.

These municipal regulations provide a framework within which private investment decisions, which are the basis for most of the development and redevelopment that occurs within a city, must be made. Such regulations include building and housing codes and public health, environmental protection, and land subdivision regulations. But perhaps the most influential in relation to the quality of the built environment are the controls over the use of land incorporated into a city's zoning ordinance.

REGULATING THE USE OF LAND

Zoning is the process through which local governments subdivide their territory into geographical districts; designate what uses can be allowed, either by right or under certain conditions, in each district; and specify the intensity at which individual parcels of land can be developed. Since it places limits upon the ways in which people can use their property, it is a process that must also have a strong legal foundation.

Constitutionally, zoning is an exercise of the police power, the power of the state to take actions that are deemed necessary to protect and advance the public health, welfare, and safety. This power is delegated by the state to its constituent local governments.

In the case of zoning, this delegation is accomplished through the passage of an enabling act by the state legislature. In most cases these acts are based on the Standard State Zoning Enabling Act, which was published by the U.S. Department of Commerce in 1926. That same year, in the case of *Village of Euclid, Ohio, v. Ambler Realty Co.*, the U.S. Supreme Court declared that zoning was a legitimate exercise of the police power by municipal governments.

Following this Supreme Court decision, the adoption of municipal zoning ordinances spread rapidly throughout the country. In most cases, these ordinances followed the approach to land use regulation which was embodied in the standard act. This approach can best be termed *prescriptive*.

Prescriptive Zoning

The fundamental principle underlying a prescriptive zoning ordinance is that urban uses and activities are incompatible with one another and should be strictly separated. In conformance with this principle, not only are residential, commercial, and industrial use categories defined, but within these categories further detailed activities are classified. Thus, single-family zones with varying density limitations are created. Duplexes and/or apartments are allowed only in specific zoning districts. Commercial and business uses are classified into several districts ranging from office parks to the central business area. And industrial districts are differentiated on the basis of such characteristics as size and type of operation.

The prescriptive approach is by far the dominant form of regulatory planning in the United States. In a recent comparative study the advantages of this approach have been described as follows:

These systems offer a written definition of all the conditions under which development may take place and are clearly based on a desire to maximize certainty. Such certainty is of two kinds. First, there is the certainty for landowners and developers. The intention is to give them an incontrovertible brief for the future use of the land and the potential for development, and thus permit them to put forward proposals with minimum risk. The second kind of certainty is for those charged with decision making. A regulatory system of control gives the least possible opportunity for decisions to be made according to whim, chance or political expediency.[1]

These are significant advantages and no doubt help to explain the pervasiveness and persistence of the prescriptive approach. They also reflect the developmental characteristics and political culture of American urban communities in the period prior to World War II. However, these factors have changed.

During the past 50 years, urban activities have multiplied considerably in type and variety. Urban political systems have become more fragmented and participatory. Economic development has become a major concern of urban policymakers, and environmental protection has become a preoccupation of many urban citizens.

The Search for Flexibility

In response to these trends, efforts have been made to introduce flexibility into the prescriptive standards and make their administration more accommodating:

What is striking about all studies of regulatory systems of planning is how widespread the attempts are to build in flexibility, either at the source in the zoning documents themselves or through negotiations. Thus the US has possibilities for flexible zoning (see Rose 1979, 147–177), which have attracted favorable comments from a British observer (Wakeford 1990). Babcock (1966) and Babcock and Siemon (1990) present us with the image of zoning as a game in which developers, municipalities, and residents seek to achieve an advantage through the manipulation of the apparent certainties of the system.[2]

Introducing flexibility at the source is achieved through the creation of new zoning districts in the ordinance itself. During the past 30 years or so, such new approaches as overlay zones, floating zones, special use districts, and provisions for planned unit developments have entered the zoning lexicon. But this has resulted in the further proliferation of use-specific zoning districts, each with its own set of rules and requirements.

Flexibility by negotiation can be accomplished in part through the rezoning process. The implementation of any development that does not fit precisely within the prescriptive use regulations, or whose location is not within the boundaries of the appropriate district, will require a zoning change. Changes to the zoning map are amendments to the zoning ordinance, and require a public hearing before the planning commission and final action by the city council. This process can provide opportunities to explore alternative ways of minimizing the adverse impacts of specific proposals and of achieving some community objective.

However, these two approaches to increasing the adaptability of prescriptive land use regulations interact in a way that increases the number and intensity of developmental conflicts. Pressures for rezoning tend to occur most frequently at the boundaries between zoning districts. More districts mean more boundaries. More boundaries mean more pressure points for change and conflict.

The prescriptive approach to zoning was designed in part to make both public and private developmental decision making predictable. Then, as such decision-making became more volatile in response to the changing nature of urban development, efforts were made to make the system more flexible. But these efforts have been incremental and have tended to aggravate the underlying problems. However, an alternative approach, known as *performance zoning,* has been formulated during the past 20 years, which offers a means of dealing with these problems.

PERFORMANCE ZONING

The first performance zoning ordinance was adopted by Bucks County, Pennsylvania, in 1974. The general principles upon which performance zoning is based were compiled into a book published in 1980.[3] During the past 15 years a small but growing number of counties and cities have adopted this approach. It is an approach that views land use regulation from a different perspective.

The fundamental concept underlying performance zoning is that within broad limits varying urban uses can coexist with one another. The key to compatibility is the intensity with which, rather than the purpose for which, land is used.

In a performance ordinance, uses are classified into general categories. The basis for these categories is shared characteristics such as traffic generation; the relative balance between land devoted to buildings and impervious surfaces, and land left in a natural state; and the intensity of the proposed activity as measured by such factors as residential density, non-residential floor space, or employment.

Since the use categories are quite broad, and the premise upon which the ordinance is based is that many uses can be made compatible with one another, the performance approach results in significantly fewer zoning districts. For an urban area there are seven basic zones, as follows:[4]

The *Rural* zone includes land which is not expected or desired to be developed for urban uses over the next 20 years or so. It is essentially a holding zone. Any development will be of very low density. If land becomes ripe for development it will be rezoned, normally to the development district described below.

The *Development District* zone allows a wide range of use categories, virtually all except agricultural or industrial. It is used to designate those areas which are intended to accommodate most of the city's planned and/or anticipated development over the next 20 years or so. Periodically, say every three to five years, land needs should be evaluated and if necessary additional areas rezoned to this district. These additional areas would come mainly from the Rural zones.

The *Estate* zone is used to delineate areas where it is desirable and/or appropriate to encourage low-density residential development. These are normally located on the outskirts of the city, and often have limited services available. They are populated by people who want a "country" type of environment in close proximity to the urban area.

The *Neighborhood Conservation* (NC) zone is applied to single-family residential areas existing at the time that the ordinance is adopted. Its purpose is to prevent such areas becoming non-conforming and to protect the present residential neighborhoods. No new NC zones are created following initial adoption. Any change within these zones is expected to occur through infill and redevelopment.

The *Commercial Conservation* zone is applied to business districts other than downtown or malls existing at the time of adoption. No expansion or creation of these zones is allowed. Change is expected only through infill and redevelopment.

The *Urban Core* zone is applied to specialized commercial areas such as downtown or major malls. While expansion is allowed, the main form of change is anticipated to be redevelopment and infilling.

The *Industrial* zone includes existing industrial areas plus the land appropriate and needed for industrial uses over the next 20 to 25 years.

The zoning districts are delineated geographically in relation to the type of change anticipated and/or planned within each part of the urban area. Periodically, about every three to five years, the map will be reviewed and revised as appropriate. These revisions mainly involve changing newly identified growth areas from the Rural to the Development District classification. The city's comprehensive plan; the availability of existing, proposed, or potential public services; and development trends and market factors will be considered in the preparation and review of the zoning map.

Within zoning districts, the intensity of potential development on a project site and actual development on adjoining parcels are measured through such factors as residential density or non-residential floor area ratios; the amount of impervious surfaces; the height and bulk of structures; the extent of exterior storage; vehicle trip generation and attraction; and the hours of operation. Based on a combination of these factors, sites will be assigned a *land use intensity* rating.

The relative ratings of the proposed and the existing uses determine what level and intensity of buffering will be required between them. A proposed project with a low rating adjoining existing uses with higher ratings will require an intensive treatment of the boundaries between them. If two adjoining uses have identical ratings, no buffering may be required. In most cases, the size of the building and of the parking area will also require that general landscaping standards be met by a proposed project.

A performance zoning ordinance also contains resource protection standards, which are used to determine the capacity of a site to absorb development. These standards relate to such natural features as floodplains, wetlands, ponds and lakes and their shorelines, drainageways, steep slopes, ravines and bluffs, mature woodlands, and prime agricultural land. The standards are used to identify which, if any, portions of such areas within a site can be built upon, graded, or regraded.

Acceptance of Performance Zoning

There is little available data concerning the number of local governments that use the performance approach. A request for information about such communities published in the newsletter of the American Institute of Certified Planners in 1993 generated information that suggested about 50 cities and counties throughout the country were using this technique.[5] This survey also suggested that in many cases these communities were not using a "pure" performance approach but were adapting the general principles to their specific needs. This was especially true of urban communities, probably since the basic performance concepts were formulated within a rural county.

Performance zoning evolved as a more effective way of encouraging environmentally sensitive and innovative development. It offers developers significantly more flexibility than prescriptive zoning. It has proved to be adaptable to a variety of local conditions, both rural and urban. So, why has it not been adopted by more communities?

To a large degree this lack of acceptance can be explained by tradition and inertia. Prescriptive zoning has been the norm for over 70 years. By the time the performance principles were being articulated in the early 1970s, most communities using zoning had already adopted an ordinance. These ordinances were based on the traditional prescriptive principles.

The weight of tradition has also been intensified by the inertia that permeates many local political systems. Policymakers are generally more comfortable with incremental and marginal changes. Overcoming the status quo, as would be required with a major overhaul of their land use regulatory system, is difficult. It requires considerable mobilization of resources, and is more likely to be approached with reluctance than enthusiasm.

In the case of zoning, these factors are aggravated by the fact that land use and developmental issues have become highly contentious in recent years. Public control over the use of private property has become the subject of considerable concern. In this context, prescriptive zoning has the relative advantage of a solid legal foundation. The model-enabling legislation and the Supreme Court decision 70 years ago establishing its constitutionality have provided support to the city attorneys who have defended local officials in subsequent litigation. Many of them would probably be uncomfortable with the task of defending a significantly different approach, and would be cautious in advising local policymakers interested in making such a change.

Factors such as these suggest that performance zoning is more likely to be accepted in a community which is adopting a zoning ordinance for the first time rather than one which is updating an existing set of regulations. Yet the city of Auburn, Alabama, was clearly in the second category when the performance concept was brought to the attention of its policymakers in the early 1980s.

ZONING IN AUBURN

Auburn's first zoning ordinance was adopted by the city council in March 1950. At that time the city was a small college town with a population of about 12,940, most of whom were students at the Alabama Polytechnic Institute (API). This prescriptive ordinance had four residential zones, two business zones, one public building zone, and one light industrial zone.

This first ordinance stayed in effect for about 20 years. In the late 1960s, the city had a comprehensive plan prepared that served as the basis for updating its land use regulations. A new zoning ordinance was adopted by the city council in December 1971. This ordinance was also prescriptive, and included eight residential, five commercial, one agricultural, one institutional, and two industrial zoning districts.

By 1970, the city's population had increased to about 22,770, the API had become Auburn University, and the students residing within the city amounted to half the total population. This second ordinance stayed in effect with minor amendments until the new performance ordinance was adopted in November 1984.

Thus, Auburn's decision-makers had used a prescriptive approach for almost 35 years. But during a period of about two years, the political leadership agreed to adopt a radically different approach to land use regulation. The impetus for this change came from a community visioning effort known as "Auburn 2000," which in turn was a response to developmental and political problems.

The Auburn 2000 Project[6]

Between 1970 and 1980, the population of Auburn increased about 26 percent, from 22,770 to 28,610. In part, this growth was caused by increases in the enrollment at Auburn University. But it also reflected even greater increases in the non-student population. Such growth generated a demand for apartments for the many students who lived off-campus, subdivisions for the non-student households, and commercial facilities to serve everyone.

The resulting expansion of the built environment was extensive but not attractive. The apartments and commercial projects consisted mainly of nondescript structures surrounded by boundary-to-boundary asphalt or concrete paving. Landscaping was nonexistent and natural features were frequently mutilated to create sites that were easy to develop. By the end of the decade the ugly results of this building boom were widespread and well remarked in a community that, due to its university orientation, had more than its share of articulate citizens, and a community whose motto was "Auburn, the loveliest village of the plains."

The drabness of the built environment was complemented by the liveliness of the political climate. The city had a hybrid government which included a manager, a mayor elected at-large, an eight-member city council, and a council president. Confusion concerning responsibilities led to bickering, fragmentation, and deadlock within the city's administration. These conditions were on public view twice a month at the council meetings, which were rated by many residents as great entertainment! However, by the end of the decade the situation was ripe for change.

In 1980, a relative newcomer to Auburn ran a grassroots campaign and was elected mayor. She ran for election determined to focus the community's attention on issues rather than the personality-based bickering that had characterized the city council during the previous term of office. In her 1980 campaign, she stressed several policy areas, including the overriding objective of restructuring the city's government, the need for greater and permanent support for the city's schools, the allocation of more resources to economic development, and the need to update the city's developmental policies and regulations. In the general election she was the leading vote-getter, and then handily beat the runner-up in the runoff election.

Following the election, the mayor-elect began considering ways of implementing her campaign promises. One of her objectives was to involve the community at-large in formulating policies for the city in her areas of concern. In concert with a number of civic leaders she developed the concept of a community-based effort and christened it "Auburn 2000."

Auburn 2000 consisted of a steering committee, eight functional subcommittees, and a technical services committee.[7] The steering committee included the mayor, the city manager, the members of the planning commission, and several administrative officials. Its role was described as follows:

Throughout the process the steering committee functioned as a "traffic cop" directing the flow of information. It reviewed draft plans, evaluated subcommittee recommendations, resolved conflicting information, and reduced the incidence of opposing recommendations.[8]

Each of the eight subcommittees consisted of 18 to 24 members and was assigned a specific aspect of the community to study: land use, housing, recreation, transportation and utilities, economic development, education, civic enrichment, and governmental organization. A member of the city council was assigned to each subcommittee to act as a liaison. The subcommittees' responsibilities were stated as follows:

The members of each subcommittee were asked to assess the present condition of the system, program, service, or function assigned to them. Having studied the existing situation, the subcommittees developed short-range recommendations for specific expansion, rehabilitation, and replacement necessary to meet the needs of the city. In addition, more comprehensive recommendations covering the period from five years to the year 2000 were made.[9]

The technical services committee consisted of 10 members, mainly faculty from Auburn University whose expertise was relevant to the concerns of one or more of the subcommittees. The city council had earlier engaged the services of a planning consulting firm from Birmingham to update its comprehensive plan, and a planner from this firm worked with the city throughout much of the process.

The organizational structure was put in place and the members of each committee and subcommittee selected and assigned by October 1982. The process began with a kick-off meeting on November 1, 1982, following which the subcommittees began their work. They used a common set of population projections, which were prepared by the planning consultant, and provided a uniform estimate of potential demand for services and facilities. They met in work sessions, held public meetings, and consulted with the members of the technical services committee and the planning consultant.

An eight-page supplement was distributed through the local newspapers which described the process, summarized the existing conditions, highlighted the areas of critical concern, and included a questionnaire which asked for readers' opinions and suggestions. Presentations to business, professional, and civic groups, and coverage of activities in the local news media kept the community informed concerning the progress of the project and the major findings and recommendations that were being formulated.

Throughout the spring of 1983, the subcommittees prepared draft reports presenting their findings, conclusions, and recommendations. These reports were submitted to the steering committee. During the summer and fall of 1983, the steering committee reviewed the draft reports submitted by the subcommittees. These reports were then combined into one document which was first reviewed by the planning commission and then presented to the city council.

With regard to changing the city's approach to guiding development, the Auburn 2000 project became a major coordinating mechanism. It brought together the concerns and recommendations of three entities—the land use subcommittee and the land use plan; the planning commission and the first draft of a new zoning ordinance; and the city council and the final version of the ordinance.

The Land Use Subcommittee

The land use subcommittee consisted of members of the Auburn planning commission and representatives of the development community. The subcommittee's charge was as follows:

The subcommittee will develop a long-range land use plan for the year 2000 and beyond. Having done so the subcommittee will analyze the city's zoning ordinance, subdivision regulations and other codes that regulate building and land development. These ordinances and regulations of the city will be assessed for their impact on land development and the subcommittee will recommend such changes as it deems appropriate to ensure orderly growth to the year 2000.[10]

The subcommittee's first efforts addressed the issue of formulating a new land use plan. The need for such a plan had already been acknowledged by planning commission members. In April 1982, the commission chairman had appointed a steering committee to guide the work of updating the plan. It consisted of himself as chair, the mayor, and two other members, one of whom later became the city's planning director.

In June 1982, this steering committee met with the planner from the consulting firm that had been engaged by the city council to assist in preparing the plan. Contact with this planner was maintained throughout the summer and fall.

In November 1982, the work of overseeing the plan preparation was assumed by the Auburn 2000 land use subcommittee. All the members of the planning commission's steering committee except the mayor, plus several other commission members, had been appointed to the land use subcommittee. The chairman of the planning commission also served as chair of the subcommittee.

The subcommittee members worked closely with the city's planning consultant, and their combined efforts resulted in a generalized land use map and a series of developmental policies for the major uses and critical areas within the city. These recommendations were transmitted to the planning commission in the fall of 1983. The land use plan was formally adopted by the planning commission in December 1983.

During the subcommittee's deliberations, especially its evaluation of the city's regulatory devices, the concept of performance zoning was introduced by the planning consultant. The consultant also discussed the performance concept with the mayor. It should also be noted that in December 1983, a member of the planning commission and of the land use subcommittee was appointed by the city manager to the position of planning director for the city.

In concluding their work, the subcommittee members recommended that the city adopt the performance zoning approach in revising the zoning ordinance and as a way of implementing its developmental policies.

THE PLANNING COMMISSION[11]

The interest of the planning commission members in the performance concept was sufficient by the late summer of 1983 that the planning consultant prepared a draft performance zoning ordinance for their consideration. This first draft was presented to the commission on October 13, 1983, and discussed in more detail on October 20, 1983.

The commission held a formal public hearing on the proposed new ordinance on November 10, 1983. This was followed by a series of working meetings at which issues of concern to various groups and neighborhood representatives were discussed. These meetings continued through the early weeks of 1984. They were public, lengthy, and devoted to the questions raised during the public hearing.

The planning commission held a second public hearing on March 8, 1984, following which further changes were made to the proposed ordinance. Then on April 12, 1984, the commission voted unanimously to recommend the proposed ordinance to the city council.

In June 1984, the city council referred the proposed ordinance back to the commission for further study. The commission held several meetings as a committee-of-the-whole for that purpose and recommended a number of changes to the original proposal. These changes were officially adopted by the commission on September 13, 1984, and sent to the council.

The City Council[12]

In April 1984, the chairman of the planning commission gave the members of the city council an overview of the commission's proposed ordinance. The council then held two work sessions in which it reviewed the draft in considerable detail.

On May 15, 1984, the proposed ordinance was introduced and given its first reading. It was then subjected to a lengthy public hearing, following which unanimous consent was denied, meaning that no action could be taken on it at that meeting.

On June 5, 1984, the council addressed the ordinance for the second time. The council president noted that the council members had been continuing their study of the proposed ordinance as a committee-of-the-whole, and had agreed that it should be referred back to the planning commission. Another lengthy public hearing followed, and then the council adopted a resolution sending the proposed ordinance back to the commission for further study.

In September 1984, as a result of the requested further study, the commission sent the council a number of recommended changes to its original proposal. On October 2, 1984, the proposed zoning ordinance with these changes was introduced. It was given its first reading, and unanimous consent was denied.

The second reading of the proposed ordinance was held on October 16, 1984. It again initiated a lengthy public hearing, at the conclusion of which the council voted to refer it to a committee-of-the-whole meeting on October 30, 1984.

On November 6, 1984, the proposed ordinance was first discussed as a report presented at a committee-of-the-whole meeting. A number of residents continued the discussion during the "citizens communications" portion of the agenda. A further committee-of-the-whole meeting was held on November 13, 1984.

On November 20, 1984, the proposed ordinance received its second reading. Yet another lengthy public hearing followed the introduction of the ordinance. The council approved a number of additional changes, and then the amended ordinance was adopted by a vote of 6 to 3.

Adapting the Performance Approach

In fashioning a performance ordinance for Auburn, the consultant did not merely copy the model ordinance. The first draft included 10 zoning districts, seven of which were basically the same as in the model ordinance and were described earlier. Three additional zones were created which related specifically to the needs and characteristics of Auburn as a growing university community. These three were as follows:

The *Holding District* was applied to the land owned by the State of Alabama (i.e., Auburn University and Chewacla State Park) and to the land surrounding Lake Ogletree owned by the Auburn Water Works Board. The state land is exempt from local zoning regulations, and the Water Works Board desired to protect the lake since it is a major source of potable water for the City.

The *University Services District* was designed to accommodate the needs of Auburn as a college town. It was applied to the area adjoining the main campus, and allows high-density residential uses plus institutional and limited commercial uses that serve the needs of students and faculty.

The *Redevelopment District* reflected the fact that Auburn contained areas in the central part of the City which were deteriorating in condition, and/or occupied by obsolete land uses. The community wished to encourage redevelopment in these areas, and this zone was intended to help achieve that purpose.

The first draft of the proposed ordinance also included an *Estate District*, a zone that was part of the model code. It was applied to an area around the airport and was intended to accommodate low-density residential development. However, the appropriateness of the zone was disputed, and it was eliminated.

There was one other significant difference between the model and the commission's proposal. In the model ordinance, the planning commission is not involved in the administration of the ordinance. A development project is reviewed by the planning staff and, if it meets the requirements of the ordinance, it is approved by the staff. The planning commission's role is to consider amendments to the text and the map, and carry out an overall review and evaluation and report to the city council at least once every five years.

In the proposed ordinance for Auburn, site plans for virtually all except single-family housing projects are reviewed by the staff, but approval of the plans is a responsibility of the planning commission. This procedure is required for both permitted and conditional uses, and the latter require a public hearing before both the commission and the city council.

This deviation from the model was clearly a procedural change desired and designed by the planning commission members. The prior prescriptive ordinance did not give the commission any administrative responsibilities except for group developments. Such projects required rezoning and the simultaneous submission and approval of a development plan. The planning commission forwarded a recommendation to the city council, and the council took the final action on any such request.

Apparently the commission members liked the procedural aspects of the group development projects and incorporated them into the proposed performance ordinance. Such procedures were perceived as providing them an opportunity to influence the design and layout of individual projects. This objective was clearly related to the widespread concern for the quality of the built environment.

Issues Raised During the Review[13]

Over a period of 14 months, the proposed ordinance had been drafted and then become the subject of four formal public hearings and numerous work sessions. There was continuous and widespread participation of the public in all of these discussions. In addition, there was extensive coverage of the debate in the local news media.

Apart from questioning changes affecting the zoning of specific parcels of property, representatives of the development professions were neither prominent nor persistent participants in this review process. Apparently there were few situations where the new zoning map created severe problems such as down-zoning. And in general, the flexibility of the performance approach was attractive. Real estate, development, and design professionals often commented that the new ordinance was difficult to read and understand.

On the other hand, there was considerable comment from the general public, most of it critical, especially from residents of the city's established single-family neighborhoods. During the course of the review, several of these neighborhoods became organized, and appointed officers and/or spokespersons to present their views and petitions.

Although expressed in many different ways, the underlying objection of these opponents was the fear of the *Development District* (DD) zone. This fear was based on the fact that the DD zone allowed virtually any uses except industrial and agricultural, and the definition of "family" was such that up to five unrelated individuals could live in a dwelling unit. This raised the specter of student apartments. And since it was intended to accommodate most of the development likely to occur over the next 20 years or so, the DD zone was applied to relatively large areas of vacant land.

These issues arose at the beginning of the review process. They could easily have derailed the process and forced the planning commission to abandon the performance approach. They were, however, addressed directly and resolved through the ability of the consultant and the commission members to adapt the performance concept to local concerns.

Responding to Community Concerns[14]

To respond to the criticisms and allay the fears concerning the DD zone, the planning commission made two major modifications to the proposed ordinance. The first response was the creation of another zone not found in the model ordinance—the *Development District–Housing* (DD-H) zone. This was designed as a low-to-medium-density residential zone, and also allows outdoor recreational and public service uses. Its purpose is defined as being:

to promote conventional and performance single family housing and/or provide a transition between the Neighborhood Conservation District (NC) and the Development District (DD).

The DD-H zone was formulated and mapped during the early months of 1984. Geographically, it was applied in the form of a

400-foot strip between an NC zone and a DD zone. In effect, it provided a protective zone around any existing single-family neighborhood which adjoined undeveloped land that was proposed to be included in a DD zone.

The definition and inclusion of the DD-H zone did not entirely satisfy the neighborhood activists because it allowed apartments. However, it was included among those zones where the definition of family virtually eliminated the possibility that such apartments would be occupied by students.

The second response related to the regulations regarding the rezoning of property. As a corollary to the addition of the DD-H zone, new language was added to the provisions specifying standards for map amendments. This language stated that:

No rezoning of land from the Rural (R) District to any other district other than the Development District–Housing (DD-H) shall be permitted within 400 feet of a Neighborhood Conservation (NC) District.

This provision was one of the changes made by the planning commission after referring the draft ordinance by the city council for further study. It had the effect of requiring a protective DDH zone around new single-family areas as well as existing ones. It appears, therefore, to have reflected the continuing concerns of the residential communities as expressed during the city council's hearings and work sessions.

Continuing Review and Revision[15]

The adoption of the ordinance was not a complete and final action. Concerns persisted and surfaced at the various times that the document was reviewed. The ordinance contains a provision that at least once every three years the planning commission shall review it and, as appropriate, recommend changes to the city council. (The model ordinance requires such review at least once every five years.) Following adoption in 1984, reviews were carried out in 1986, 1987, 1988, 1990, and 1991. Thereafter, the commission began reviewing every three years. These reviews resulted in some significant changes.

In 1987, a provision was added that allowed the creation of new NC zones adjoining existing NC zones, provided that such a new zone had a maximum density equal to or less than that of the existing zone. A second provision was added that if all the owners in an existing or proposed single-family subdivision located in any R, DD, DD-H, or RDD districts petitioned for an NC designation, it could be granted. In 1988, the description of the purpose of the NC zone was amended to recognize the creation of new NC zones.

All these amendments significantly changed the purpose of the NC zoning district from that envisioned in the model ordinance. New NC zones could now be created. This in itself might not be a problem, but the conditions placed on the zoning of property adjacent to NC zones had important ramifications.

The ordinance restricted the rezoning of property within 400 feet of an NC zone to DD-H, or to an NC designation of equivalent or lower maximum density. This limitation was aggravated by the fact that the original zoning map included substantial areas of the city in the R zone. This was especially true of the southern portion of the city. This area contained large amounts of vacant buildable land. Beginning in the latter part of the 1980s, it became a major growth area, absorbing most of the new single-family housing.

As development occurred in such R areas, the performance zoning principles indicated that they should be rezoned to DD. However, many of the new residential areas in Auburn were rezoned to an NC designation. The resulting patchwork of NC zones had the potential to inhibit non-residential development and confine new residential subdivisions to equivalent or lower densities than those existing. The latter result was at odds with the goal of creating the varied residential neighborhoods enunciated in the Auburn 2000 plan.

These problems were discussed in a report from the planning commission to the city council prepared as part of the first triannual review in September 1993. Subsequently, in May 1994, the city council, acting on recommendations of the planning commission, amended the ordinance to eliminate the restrictions on rezoning property adjacent to single-family subdivisions. Such restrictions were replaced with requirements setting a minimum distance from single-family property boundaries that structures in adjoining zones could be placed, and requiring additional buffering. Thus, the prior limitation on adjacent uses and density was replaced with increased dimensional and buffering standards.

At the same time, the ordinance was amended to include a new zone. Called the *Limited Development District* (LDD) zone, it is intended to accommodate relatively low-density residential development with a maximum density of about two dwelling units per acre. It also allows neighborhood shopping centers at specific locations subject to some design standards. It is generally equivalent to the Estate District in the model ordinance.

In the 1996 triannual review, considerable attention was focused on the zoning map. Substantial areas zoned R were recommended for rezoning to LDD. This was also in part a corrective measure, in recognition of the over-zoning of R districts in the original map. It brought Auburn's ordinance even more into conformity with the principles of the model performance ordinance.

Conditions and Strategies Supporting Change

Excluding the initial discussions of the underlying concept and principles, the performance zoning ordinance was adopted by the Auburn city council about 13 months after it was first introduced. Given the substantial differences between the prior prescriptive and the present performance regulations, this change was accomplished in a relatively short time. A number of factors contributed to this result.

1. The performance concept was inherently sound. It was well developed and documented. It had been applied successfully in other communities. It was not an "off the wall" untested idea.

2. The concept was strongly advocated and well explained by the city's planning consultant. The people mainly responsible for presenting it to the community and its political leaders understood it and could explain it effectively to other people.

3. The idea surfaced at a time when the new mayor had formulated a political platform in which new approaches to community planning and development were an important plank. The performance concept

was entirely consistent with this platform and the mayor became a powerful advocate of it.

4. Through the Auburn 2000 project, the performance concept was endorsed and espoused by the land use subcommittee and the planning commission. It was presented to the community with such support and had to be taken seriously.

5. The groundwork for public discussion of the concept was laid through the Auburn 2000 process. Subsequently, adequate opportunity for public discussion was provided both by the planning commission and by the city council. This discussion evolved into a dialog. Questions and issues raised by community representatives were fully addressed by the commission and council members.

6. As the dialog continued, most of the issues were resolved, and the points of contention were gradually reduced essentially to one—namely, the general fear of the Development District zone and the need to protect the single-family neighborhoods from its perceived harmful impacts.

7. The commission was able to fashion a satisfactory response to this final community concern. This response, the creation of the Development District–Housing zone, preserved the intent of the performance approach but also directly addressed the concerns of the neighborhoods.

8. Throughout the entire process the mayor, the commission members, and the planning director stood firmly behind the performance concept. They remained clearly committed to it throughout countless hours of contentious argument. Yet they were not so rigid in their advocacy that they could not consider and conceive compromises in details that would make the overall approach acceptable.

In retrospect, performance zoning in Auburn was introduced into an environment that was initially unreceptive. In reacting to this situation, its proponents pressed hard to get the concept accepted and then tried to get as many of the details as possible adopted. Following adoption, they have worked hard to make the ordinance work and to draw attention to its positive impact on the built environment. And they have used the required review process as the means to gradually but systematically incorporate selected elements that are important in relation to the performance approach but that had to be sacrificed to get the proposed ordinance adopted.

CONCLUSION

This change in the city's approach to regulatory planning was not, nor can it be adequately treated as, an isolated happening. It was one of several changes in the structure and functions of the city's government which gained momentum from the Auburn 2000 project.

For example, in 1984 the city created its own economic development department and initiated a proactive and comprehensive program aimed at increasing non-university employment opportunities. In 1983, voters approved changing the hybrid form of government to a true council-manager system, and this went into effect in 1986. Substantial, and steadily increasing, funds have been appropriated each year by the city council to help improve the city's school system.

These and many other changes have been both a cause and an effect of the increasing professionalism among the city's personnel. And they have produced tangible results. During the past 10 years the city has conducted an annual citizens survey every spring. Throughout this period an average of 86 percent of the city's households have consistently rated the level of public services they receive as either excellent or good.[16]

With regard to the built environment, the new performance zoning ordinance has had visible impacts. Few people today would dispute the claim that there is an observable difference between projects that predate and those that were built following implementation of the current performance standards. The former are drab and uninviting. The latter are landscaped and fit comfortably within both the built and the natural environments.

The triannual review process has become institutionalized and offers the community, as well as the planning commission and the council, an opportunity to evaluate the impact of the performance principles on actual development. Further changes have been made in the provisions of the ordinance as a result. Some of these bring the regulations more into conformity with the performance model. But such conformity is not slavish; it is aimed at principles, not particulars. Other changes have been made which respond specifically to the conditions and opportunities unique to Auburn.

Issues still remain to be addressed. Some segments of the com-

munity are pressing for even more stringent landscaping requirements and the addition of design standards. The development
community is increasingly questioning the administrative role that
the planning commission fashioned for itself.

Overall, the adoption of the performance approach is now
viewed as a positive change. The new ordinance is considered to
be one of the elements which, during the past decade, has helped
Auburn earn a reputation as a well-run and attractive community
whose leaders are responsive to needs and opportunities rather
than inhibited by habit and tradition.

NOTES

1. Philip Booth, "Zoning or Discretionary Action: Certainty and Re-
sponsiveness in Implementing Planning Policy," *Journal of Planning Education and Research* 14, no. 2 (Winter 1995): 104.

2. Ibid.

3. Lane Kendig, *Performance Zoning* (Chicago: Planners Press, American Planning Association, 1980).

4. Ibid., pp. 110–115.

5. Based on responses to a request published in the informal newsletter of the American Institute of Certified Planners distributed in December
1992.

6. The discussion of the background for the Auburn 2000 project is
based on discussions with the mayor, city manager, former members of
the planning commission and planning director, and former chairman of
the planning commission; on minutes of the city and the planning commission; and on newspaper reports.

7. Auburn 2000, *Comprehensive Plan for Auburn, Alabama* (Auburn,
AL: Auburn 2000, 1983), p. 5.

8. Ibid., p. 4.

9. Ibid.

10. Mayor's office, Auburn, Alabama, *Planning for the Future*, no date;
a newspaper supplement describing the Auburn 2000 project.

11. This section is based on the minutes of the Auburn city planning
commission for 1983 and 1984.

12. This section is based on the minutes of the city council of the city
of Auburn for 1984.

13. This section is based on the records of public hearings, and the
minutes of the Auburn planning commission and city council.

14. This section is based on the minutes and other records of the Au-

burn city planning commission, and on the various drafts of the proposed zoning ordinance.

15. This section is based on the annual and triannual reviews carried out by the Auburn city planning commission.

16. City of Auburn, Alabama, *Citizens Survey* (Auburn, AL: Reports of the annual citizens surveys for 1986 through 1995).

6

Providing the American Dream

T. PHILLIP DUNLAP

In the early 1990s, Rock Hill, South Carolina, had an inadequate supply of housing for its low- and moderate-income families. However, this city of 44,000 population had earned a strong reputation for its long-range planning and innovative approaches to solving community problems. In particular, the city's leaders were dedicated to the improvement of the lives of the city's less fortunate citizens.[1] This concern was shared by the city manager.

City manager Joe Lanford had a background in urban planning. When he became city manager, after serving as the assistant to the long-time city manager Max Holland, one of his first concerns was to initiate a new planning process. Lanford realized that the city had to be prepared if it was to take advantage of the opportunity for a prosperity created by the expansion of the Charlotte metropolitan area. With this in mind, he initiated a strategic planning effort known as Empowering the Vision (ETV).

ETV assumed that the city government would play a major role in molding the community's future growth and direction. It emphasized downtown revitalization, education, and commercial growth. But Lanford also knew that ETV had to address the needs of low- and moderate-income neighborhoods if it was to have the broad-based community support it needed to be successful.

Professor Craig Wheeland described the political situation in Rock Hill at this time in the following terms:

[C]ommunity politics since the early 1970s have centered on the proposed solutions to several main problems: the decline of the textiles industry; the decline of downtown; the influx of many new residents, who have raised the city's population nearly 25 percent since 1980; the threat of Rock Hill's becoming just another suburb in the growing Charlotte metropolitan area; and the need to secure the participation of the African American community, which was one-third of Rock Hill's 1990 population of 44,000.[2]

Lanford felt that an affordable housing program specifically addressing the need of the African American community for improved housing opportunities would help secure its support for the other elements of ETV.

The 1990 General Plan for Rock Hill recommended that most of the anticipated growth should take place in defined development areas, each having a focal point or magnet for development. Clinton Junior College, located at Crawford Road and Heckle Boulevard, is one of the focal points of the Crawford Road Development Area. The area was chosen as the likely starting point for an affordable housing initiative.

Focal point planning, in contrast to comprehensive planning, addresses a specific issue or issues in a defined geographic area. The Crawford Road Development Area was developed in an effort to improve housing, increase employment opportunities, and upgrade the transportation system. The Crawford Road Development Area Plan is an attempt to define what public policies and programs will provide opportunities for residents of the area to improve their quality of life.

The private sector also benefits from the plan because it contains detailed public policies and courses of action which can be utilized by private developers to plan and implement individual projects. An essential part of the focal point planning process is the provision of specific assurances by both the public and private sectors that the plan will be followed.

The City of Rock Hill had several major problems to overcome in the preparation of the Crawford Road Development Area Plan.

Between 1980 and 1987, the Crawford Road area had grown only 1 percent in population while the entire city population had grown by 8 percent. There had been very little new housing construction by the private sector in this neighborhood. The decline in federal housing assistance programs by the early 1990s made it obvious that the city would have to play a major role in the development of decent and affordable housing in this area.

The Crawford Road Development Area Plan also identified significant problems, such as a poor connection to the city's transportation system, an inadequate local street system, and non-conforming land uses. While the plan also cited job creation as a goal, the authors of the plan recognized that this would be difficult to do because of the general residential character of this area.

The city manager decided to use the development of affordable housing as the primary means of addressing the Crawford Road area's needs. In addition to new housing, the plan called for infrastructure improvements, such as street construction and drainage facilities, to improve the overall quality of the neighborhood.

Rock Hill's managers began to analyze the best means of developing affordable housing within the target area. After studying several programs, the city elected to retain the services of a consultant to formulate an affordable housing program in cooperation with the manager, assistant manager, and planning director that would enable the city of Rock Hill to build new housing within the Crawford Road Development Area as well as other target areas. The consultant's charge was to design a program that was consistent with the statement of purpose adopted by the city council. It was the desire of the city of Rock Hill to strive to provide safe, decent, sound, and affordable housing, creating a suitable living environment for all its citizens based on the following guidelines:

1. To develop property that is largely undeveloped, eliminating conditions which could be detrimental to the public welfare.
2. To increase the tax base through property improvements.
3. To utilize the infrastructure already in place.
4. To create a low/moderate-income community.
5. To stabilize the community by making it productive.

6. To encourage developers to enter the area.

7. To equip units with electric heat pumps for heating and cooling.

8. To enhance the city's effort to revitalize the targeted community, in accordance with the already adopted Crawford Road focal point plan.

9. To utilize the existing policy on dilapidated housing to remove abandoned structures and replace with new structures.

10. To stimulate population growth within the development area.[3]

THE PROGRAM DESIGN

In accord with the city's purpose and policies, the consultant designed the program to be operated by a non-profit neighborhood-based corporation as defined in the community development block grant regulations of the federal government. The corporation actively markets the program through newspaper, television, and radio public service announcements in designated target areas within the city. The corporation governing body includes residents in the target areas.

The corporation's staff pre-screens applicants for participation in the program. Those qualifying under the program have to have a total annual adjusted gross income of not more than 80 percent of the community's median income based on family size, and they have to have the ability to make a downpayment of $500. Prospective purchasers make application to the corporation for a second mortgage loan. At this time, the corporation staff is responsible for pre-screening applicants to determine eligible candidates. Eligible applicants are then referred to a participating bank for further credit evaluation. The lending institution retains credit approval on all applications for mortgage assistance.

Community development funds received by the city are used by the corporation to establish a second mortgage loan pool and to acquire lots for housing construction. Community development funds are used to assist qualified applicants in paying the closing costs for purchase of the home. In addition, the corporation utilizes community development funds to provide low-interest construction financing to builders participating in the program. This financing enables the corporation to limit the maximum sales price of the unit and to designate where the units are built.

HOME OWNERSHIP LOAN POOL

The corporation established a home ownership loan pool consisting of commitments from private banks as well as from the state housing finance authority. Local banks interested in opportunities to address the needs of low- and moderate-income households in order to meet the requirements of the community reinvestment act (CRA)—which requires local banks to reinvest in their communities—realized the value of this program to the community and to the banks. The state housing finance authority already had low interest mortgages available to assist low and moderate income households and was willing to participate in Rock Hill's program.

Prospective purchasers have the option of financing their houses under either of two plans: (1) through the state housing finance authority or (2) through local banks. The corporation can also use community development block grant (CDBG) funds to provide eligible households with second mortgage loans up to $8,500 at a 3 percent interest rate. The maximum selling price for units under the program was established by the city at $45,000. This total included the required $500 downpayment, the first mortgage permanent loan, and the second mortgage loan provided by the corporation. Lots and closing costs were given as a grant to the buyers.

The following table illustrates how this program works for a purchaser of a home with a first mortgage with the state agency or the bank:

Sales Price	Less D.P.	Less CDBG 2nd Mortgage	1st Mortgage Needed	Monthly Payment
$45,000	($500)	($8,500)	$36,000	$290

The city developed specific guidelines for the lending institutions that wanted to participate in the affordable housing program:

1. Make at least three loans per year on a fixed rate basis for 30 years at 1 percent below the prevailing market rate.

2. Charge no origination fee or discount points on loans.

3. Provide funds for first mortgage financing on loans ranging up to $36,000 each. Small loans may be acceptable.

4. Set up necessary escrow accounts for taxes and insurance.

5. Notify housing services (a city agency) of status of each proposed borrower(s) (i.e., whether approved or rejected).

6. Request through housing services appraisals, title report, title insurance, survey if needed, and incidental loan packaging documentation.

7. Coordinate closing with the borrower(s).

8. Service loans on a month-to-month basis.

9. Notify housing services if the loan is foreclosed and request assistance in the resale of property. Housing services will in turn notify the corporation of such foreclosure.

10. Notify potential borrower(s) of decision to accept or reject loan application.

MAKING HOUSING AFFORDABLE

The primary advantage of the affordable housing program is that the downpayment and monthly payments for eligible applicants are greatly reduced. If conventional financing were used to build a home costing $45,000, the prospective buyer would be required to make a downpayment of $2,250, and pay closing costs and lot costs totaling at least another $2,500. The monthly payments for the balance of $42,750 at a prevailing rate of approximately 10.5 percent would total approximately $390.

By contrast, the affordable housing program cost eligible buyers only $500 for a downpayment and no closing or lot costs. The monthly payment was reduced from $390 to approximately $326 per month (first mortgage of $36,000 at 9 percent = $290 a month and a second mortgage of $8,500 at 3 percent = $36 a month).

CONDITIONS OF A CORPORATION'S SECOND MORTGAGE LOAN

As stated above, the second mortgage loan is granted to eligible applicants who have been approved for a first mortgage loan by a participating private sector bank. The term of the second mortgage runs concurrently with and commences on the same date as the first mortgage. The payment period will not exceed 30 years. Security for the second mortgage includes a second lien on the dwelling and land. The second mortgage loan is also not transferable.

The principal of the second mortgage loan, plus interest, is due and payable upon the sale or refinancing or transfer of the home. The second mortgage is also due and payable upon a default on the first mortgage.

SELECTION OF BUILDERS

A critical element of the program design is that the corporation builds the units by using private sector builders. The corporation selects builders through a request for proposal (RFP) process. The RFP encourages prospective builders who are "full service"—that is, those who can both build and sell the home. The RFP process requires that the builder provide a house plan and cost breakdown of the unit he proposes to build. This enables the corporation to select the unit that it feels is most desirable and, at the same time, allows it to control the cost of the unit. This process also produces a list of house plans from which prospective applicants may select their home.

Another means to lower the per unit cost involves establishing a revolving construction financing pool. These funds are used to provide zero percent interest to the selected builders. The use of this construction financing pool is important, because the corporation establishes a maximum sales price of the house and also limits the amount of profit the builder can make on the unit.

Once the unit is sold, the construction loan is paid back to the corporation, which may then be lent to other builders to construct other units, or to other eligible applicants for second mortgage loans.

PROGRAM SAFEGUARDS

In order to assure that this program will operate in an efficient manner, the corporation adopted the following safeguards:

1. The maximum selling price for a housing unit under this program will be $45,000.
2. The second mortgage shall not exceed $8,500.
3. Once applicants have been approved for a first mortgage:
   a. They will meet with an approved builder and select the unit they

wish to construct. They will then execute a sales contract with the eligible builder. This contract along with a closing statement, a commitment letter from a qualified mortgage lender, and an anticipated closing date will be forwarded to the corporation for final approval of the second mortgage.

    b. The corporation will issue a firm letter of commitment to approve the second mortgage. This letter will be placed in the applicant's file with an original forwarded to the participating bank issuing the first mortgage loan.

    c. The first mortgage lender will be responsible for closing the first and second mortgage loans on the closing date.

4. All building plans must comply with Federal Housing Administration/Veterans Administration (FHA/VA) regulations. In addition, all units must comply with all city codes and ordinances applicable to new construction.

5. The corporation will provide low interest construction financing to builders selected to participate in the program. This construction financing will be repaid the corporation at closing of the permanent loans.

6. The builder will be required to sign a legally binding commitment under which the builder agrees to:

    a. Construct or cause the construction of a new single-family detached home in accordance with the agreed-upon schedule at a total cost not to exceed $36,000.

    b. Limit its profit and overhead to amounts equivalent to those indicated in the estimated costs.

    c. Guarantee completion of the homes awarded.

    d. Assure that FHA/VA appraisals are obtained and that construction of the unit meets standards of FHA or VA.

7. The builder will also be required to submit monthly reporting forms to the corporation providing information concerning jobs, taxes, and expenditures generated as a result of the affordable housing program. In addition, the builder will make available all information pertaining to the house that may from time to time be requested by the corporation.

8. Construction will begin on all units awarded within one (1) month of commitment. Each unit must be completed within three (3) months of commitment. Units not completed by that time will be transferred to the corporation for completion. If the unit has to be completed by the corporation, the builder shall forfeit all rights to a construction profit. Evidence of start of construction will be in the form of a city building

permit, and evidence of completion will be satisfied by a city-issued occupancy permit.

9. The builder will receive a 10 percent profit on the construction of the unit. The 10 percent is based strictly on hard cost invoices. Construction advances will be made on a monthly basis. Work performed will be inspected by the housing coordinator to ensure it is in line with advances made to date. Profit due the builder will be paid at the permanent loan closing.

HOUSING COUNSELING

Once a prospective buyer has been approved for purchase of a unit, the corporation requires the applicant to participate in a housing counseling program. This program is essential to ensure that the prospective buyer fully understands the "ins and outs" of home ownership.

During the counseling sessions, prospective buyers are introduced to real estate and mortgage terminology and to the process used by lending and credit agencies. They learn how to establish a family budget and manage their money. And they are taught how to maintain their house and operate it in an energy-efficient manner.

ADVANTAGES OF AFFORDABLE HOUSING PROGRAM

The affordable housing program offers several advantages to the citizens of Rock Hill. First and most importantly, it allows residents who are now renting and unable to buy a home an opportunity to become homeowners.

Second, the program is a public-private partnership that is designed to complement both sectors' efforts and abilities to promote affordable housing. Banks making first mortgage loans decide on all credit decisions and collect the payments for themselves as well as for the non-profit corporation. The non-profit corporation provides the second mortgage loan, purchases lots for prospective buyers, provides closing costs to the buyers, and makes low-interest construction loans to builders.

The third advantage is that payments from the second mortgages are recycled into the second mortgage loan pool. After the corporation completes just 20 homes, these monthly payments alone would be enough to provide another second mortgage to a prospective new buyer.

A fourth advantage is that this program has helped to revitalize neighborhoods within the target areas and complements other revitalization efforts underway by the city, such as drainage installation, housing rehabilitation efforts, and street construction.

A fifth advantage is that once-vacant lots have been improved, with the city of Rock Hill benefiting from additional property taxes and utility fees.

A final advantage is that the program may be expanded to meet the housing needs of other income groups not now being met by conventional financing methods. In 1990, the average cost of a new home in Rock Hill was in excess of $80,000. There is a substantial market of would-be homeowners who are not able to afford the $800-plus monthly payments required of a home in that price range. Over the life of the affordable housing program, construction of units costing between $45,000 and $75,000 may be feasible to address the needs of these other income groups.

CONCLUSION

Rock Hill's approach to providing adequate housing for its low- and moderate-income residents gained support from the African American community and the business community. The effort to bring economic activity to the Crawford Road area was based on a partnership among the community, the city government, and businesses, primarily banks and builders. All these groups were winners in this program. The community enjoyed the benefit of newly constructed housing where previously were vacant lots. Families were able to move from poor housing conditions into a new home. The banks were able to invest in safe deals because of the large second mortgages provided by the city. The banks also were able to meet their requirements under the community reinvestment act with very little risk. The city also benefited in several ways. New housing was added to the tax rolls, the community was not allowed to deteriorate, and support for the Empowering the

Vision long-range strategic plan was secured. This unique approach to community problem solving proved to be beneficial for all involved.

NOTES

1. Craig M. Wheeland, "A Profile of a Facilitative Mayor: Mayor Betty Jo Rhea of Rock Hill, South Carolina," in James H. Svara and Associates, *Facilitative Leadership in Local Government* (San Francisco: Jossey-Bass Publishers, 1994).

2. Ibid.

3. City of Rock Hill, South Carolina, Affordable Housing Program Guidelines, 1992.

7

Conflict Comes to Daphne

DOUGLAS J. WATSON AND
WENDY L. HASSETT

In the late 1980s, Daphne, Alabama, adopted the council-manager form of government but abandoned it four years later. The effort to bring innovative changes to the way this quaint small city on the Alabama coast had been operated for decades did not succeed for many reasons that are explored in this case study. For an innovation as comprehensive as a change in the form of a city's government to be successful it must be carefully nurtured. The change in Daphne was made with little public involvement, and was the source of constant conflict for the four years of its use in Daphne.

In 1960, Daphne was a small town of 1,527 residents on the eastern shore of Mobile Bay in the southernmost county of Alabama. By 1970, the town had grown to 2,382 residents and by 1980, Daphne's population had expanded to 3,406. In 1988, with the estimated population of the town at 3,800, the city council decided to ask the state legislature for permission to annex three areas outside the city limits that were more than double the size of Daphne.

A local legislator introduced a bill in the legislature to accomplish three things. First, an annexation election was to be held allowing the residents of the areas outside Daphne to decide whether they wanted to become part of the city. Interestingly, the bill that passed the legislature did not allow the residents of Daphne to vote on the question. Second, a city manager was to be hired by the new council. The question of changing the form of government to council-manager was not to be determined by the voters of Daphne but was to be mandated by the legislature at the request of the incumbent governing body. Third, the new council was to be expanded to seven members elected from districts, replacing a five-member council elected at-large.

Act No. 88–615 was passed by the legislature and signed into law by the governor on May 18, 1988. It called for an annexation election in the unincorporated areas not less than 20 days nor more than 40 days from the date of enactment. Furthermore, it changed the form of government in Daphne:

> The governing body of the city of Daphne shall consist of a mayor-council-city manager. The mayor shall be elected at large, represent the city at all ceremonial functions and have veto power over all ordinances and resolutions of a general and permanent nature. The council shall consist of seven (7) members elected by districts in compliance with the Voting Rights Act of 1964. The council shall exercise the legislative functions of the city, shall have power to appoint and remove a city manager, board, commission and/or committee member, to establish other administrative departments, to distribute the work of such departments and promulgate rules and regulations for the operation thereof.
>
> The council shall be presided over by a president elected by a majority vote of the council members and the president of the council shall be a voting member of the council.
>
> The city manager shall be the head of the administrative branch of the municipal government responsible to the council for the proper administration of all affairs of the municipality.[1]

Since its incorporation as a town, Daphne had operated under a weak mayor-council form of government, with the mayor serving as the chief administrator and as the presiding member of the city council. The incumbent mayor in 1988 had served on the council since 1952 and had been mayor for three terms. The five-member council had been elected at-large, with two black council members.[2] The small town, prior to the annexation, was 43 percent minority and after the election only 15 percent. The areas to be annexed were obviously overwhelmingly white.

Interestingly, Act No. 88–615 stated: "If a majority of the votes cast in the election are in favor of annexation, the provisions of this act shall become operative at noon on the 30th day after such election. If the majority of the votes cast are against annexation, this act shall have no further effect." Since the residents of Daphne were not allowed to vote on the question of annexation, the people who lived in the unincorporated area had the ability to choose the form of government under which Daphne was to operate.

The annexation referendum was held in June 1988 in the three unincorporated areas. Those voting for the annexation numbered 560; those voting against numbered 550. After the council held a special meeting to hear protests from two residents who felt the election was not properly conducted, the mayor stated that the referendum "could have been better but I don't think it was dishonest." Despite threats from some residents to challenge the election results in court, the five-day period for contesting the election passed without anyone filing a protest. An attorney hired by one group of residents from the newly annexed area noted that his clients would have liked to challenge the election but did not have the necessary funds "to fight city hall."

The next step in the annexation process was to seek approval of the United States Justice Department under terms of the Voting Rights Act of 1965. However, before the plan could be sent to the Justice Department, the city council had to agree on a districting plan. After holding numerous public hearings and studying 11 separate proposals, the council members had a very difficult time agreeing on any one plan:

Disgruntled Daphne residents filed out of city hall after Monday night's council meeting, many angry at the council's failure to select a map for the new seven single-member districts. There was also a surprise when a councilman gave first reading to a resolution which would ask the legislature to repeal the Daphne annexation bill if no decision could be reached on the maps at the next council meeting.

Nearly 100 residents attended the three and one-half hour meeting, which began with regular council business, recessed into a third public hearing, and reconvened back into regular session.[3]

At the next meeting of the council, the mayor urged the members to adopt one of the plans: "Out of 11, I'm sure that no one map would satisfy everyone." After some discussion, the mayor's proposal was passed on a four to two vote. It took over a month for the council to approve an ordinance that officially adopted the map and allowed the city to send it to the Justice Department for approval.

Despite the pleas of a black community activist for residents to write letters to the Justice Department to strike down the results of the annexation because it diluted black voting strength, the Justice Department did approve the annexation 60 days after the plan was submitted to it by Daphne officials. So nine months after the annexation election, Daphne officials had cleared all the hurdles needed to implement the provisions of Act 88–615.

Elections had been scheduled in Daphne for August 1988, just two months after the annexation/form of government referendum. Since there was not enough time to obtain approval from the Justice Department for the new electoral arrangement, the city council asked the attorney general of Alabama whether the election should be delayed until the full legal process could be completed. The attorney general replied:

At a referendum held on June 21, 1988, the annexation to the City of Daphne provided for in Act 88–615 was approved. Therefore, no municipal election is to be held on August 23, 1988. The incumbent officials are to hold office until their successors are elected and qualified under the provisions of Act 88–615.

In March 1989, the incumbent council passed an ordinance that allowed the city to begin advertising for a city manager. The long-term mayor, who would later play a key role in dismantling council-manager government in Daphne, expressed support for the plan in an in-depth newspaper interview in early April. He said, "I like the idea of a city manager but I wish we would have had the option of hiring one, instead of it being mandated." Since the mayor was head of the city council that passed the resolution requesting the legislature to enact 88–615, his statement to the press was curious.[4] In a later interview after he left office, the mayor said he did not really understand what he and the other council members were doing at the time they requested the change in the form of government, even though the council was unanimous in requesting Act 88–615.

In the April 1989 newspaper interview, the mayor commented on the role of mayor in the new form of government:

> The new mayor is not going to be able to just sit back and draw a check. There's too much to do. People will still be calling the mayor when they have problems and they expect an answer. I see the mayor of any town as the link between the people and the governing body . . . [he should] not just be kissing babies and cutting ribbons.
>
> If I'm elected, I plan to get with the attorneys at the Alabama League of Municipalities and find out just what the law will allow.[5]

Finally, the election that was to be held the prior August was scheduled for May 9, 1989. In addition to having its population nearly tripled and changing the form of government to council-manager, Daphne was also electing its council members by district for the first time. Six candidates declared for the at-large position of mayor and at least two candidates ran for each of the council seats. In three of the new districts, there were five candidates vying for the one position on the council, with a total of 34 citizens expressing an interest in serving on the new council.

There were only three council members chosen by the voters without a runoff in the election. A local attorney, who was a strong backer of council-manager government, led the balloting for mayor by 13 votes over the long-term incumbent. Since neither had a majority of the vote, they faced each other in a runoff three weeks later. In the runoff, the incumbent mayor received 53 percent of the votes. Only one of the seven new members of the city council was an incumbent from the former at-large, five-member council.

DAPHNE'S FIRST CITY MANAGER

On June 12, the newly-elected city council was sworn into office and named a local resident as the temporary city manager. The temporary city manager, who held a Ph.D. in Finance and had recently left employment with one of the major universities in the state, immediately assumed a high profile. According to the mayor, he was a close personal friend of the council member who had been chosen by his peers to serve as the president of the city council. On the question of hiring a new fire chief, the temporary city manager told the press:

No more limbo. Enough of limbo. They as a fire department need to know where they stand with the city administration. I suspect the council is going to want me to move very quickly in that. Unless there's an objection by the council, I suspect that we'll take some action on that in the near future.

In a lengthy interview with the press, the temporary city manager explained by using the corporate analogy how the new system would work in Daphne. He concluded that the "voters really made out this time. The form of government is great and we've got the right professional personalities in the right slots." He praised the incumbent mayor as someone who would play a vital part in the new form of government. The mayor would be a "conciliator, coordinator, and negotiator" and would be called on to share his vast experience about the city with the manager and the new city council.

The city council advertised the position of city manager in four major newspapers in the state and received 40 applications. Since Alabama does not have a strong council-manager tradition[6] and since none of the cities in which the newspapers are located have city managers, the pool of professional local managers was limited. On July 12, one month after taking office, the council interviewed four candidates and decided to name the temporary city manager to the permanent position. The council president announced that all four of the candidates were good but that the temporary manager was a "benefit to us (the council) and the city of Daphne." Another member of the council declared: "I feel we have a really great city manager."

The city manager immediately took bold steps to implement the new form of government. In rather an unusual political move, he discussed his plans for the upcoming budget with the local press six days prior to introducing the budget to the city council. Most interesting about this move was that he was recommending a steep increase in the local sales tax: "I intend to recommend to the city council, effective October 1, increases in the sales tax rate for the city of Daphne" from one cent on each dollar sold by retailers to two and one-half cents. He then detailed his recommendations for "big-ticket items" that would be purchased with the increased revenue.

Within one week, he recommended to the council that city hall be expanded by 1,100 square feet to accommodate a new computer network that "will bring the city's administrative and financial controls to a level of current technology." The new city manager also established "city manager after hours" sessions twice a month for citizens who were interested in discussing issues with him. He commented to the press that "the council and city manager have asked and asked for input and we can't even get people to the forums we hold after hours." There is no evidence in the record that any of the elected officials were discussing issues publicly; apparently they were content to allow the new city manager to take the lead on the tax issue and other initiatives.

In early September 1989, the city council passed on first reading the budget presented to it by the city manager, including the 150 percent increase in the sales tax. Several business leaders expressed to the council their concerns about the sales tax increase and said their customers were "very aroused about this." The mayor told the press that the city was moving too quickly and that there was no need to have such a sharp increase in the sales tax: "I think some things could be put off for a short while; as much as a year."

During the two-week break before the second meeting in September, at which the city council would consider the budget on second reading, the mayor informed the council members by internal memorandum that he would veto the tax increase if they passed it. The mayor released the memorandum to the press at the same time he placed it in the mailboxes of the council members at city hall, so several of the council members first heard of the veto from the newspaper. The mayor said he would veto the sales tax because "of my own personal feelings" and based on the numerous complaints he received from citizens throughout the community. He said the city was moving "in too rapid a pace" and that: "I have great concern for our small business people. It's not going to affect people in higher income brackets, but there are so many people in town I know in fixed income positions."

The city manager again spoke for the council by way of a statement to the press:

> The city council and the office of the city manager release information to the press generically and in the form of interviews or official press releases, therefore, I choose not to comment on an internal memorandum from the mayor to the city council regarding the mayor's veto of the sales tax increase. I do not believe my office should break the confidence of an internal memorandum.

The mayor's veto of the sales tax increase was the first visible split to surface between the mayor and the council and city manager. However, several days after the mayor's veto and on receipt of an anonymous tip, the press accused the council of holding a secret meeting in city hall on a Sunday night to discuss the veto and other matters. The council president said the meeting did not violate the sunshine law (a state law that requires all meetings to be open to the public) because it was not a council meeting but an informal work session. Another member said he did not think it was illegal because "the lights were on and the doors were open and anyone who wanted to was welcome to attend." The mayor told the press he had not been invited to the meeting and he had his "suspicions about what they talked about," alluding to the veto of the sales tax increase, according to the press. The city attorney also said he was not invited but it was his opinion that if the doors were unlocked, the meeting was not in violation of the state's sunshine law.

At the council meeting the next night, the council voted 5 to 2 to override the mayor's veto and institute the city manager's recommendation to increase the sales tax. Two of the members attempted to reduce the size of the increase to one percent and when they failed, they voted to uphold the mayor's veto.

In the same issue of the newspaper that reported on the council's override of the mayor's veto on the sales tax increase, the city manager announced on behalf of the city's utility board that the board members had followed his recommendation to increase the water and sewer rates by approximately 10 percent. One local businessman told the paper that "I just don't think it's justified. I just think they're taking advantage of businesses" and that the city utility was "getting more than enough from business."

In November 1989, the city council approved the city manager's proposal to contract with one of the state's largest banks to issue $8 million in municipal bonds to build a new justice center and two new fire stations, for extensive street paving and storm drainage improvements, and to purchase new vehicles. The city manager announced that no referendum was required, and he ensured citizens that he had received the best possible interest rate and construction costs. At the same meeting, the council voted to activate the city's police jurisdiction that required the city to provide police and fire services and collect taxes for property within a three-mile radius of the city limits.

During this time, the council had decided to limit the mayor's involvement in several ways. According to the mayor, the council removed his name from the list of city officials who could sign checks for the city, removed him as a member of the planning commission, and did not invite him to any called meetings of the council. The mayor, however, was not content to sit on the sidelines. He suggested to the council that it may want to delay the issuance of the bonds because he had recently met with the state attorney general who had questioned the constitutionality of the city's form of government. The mayor told the council that he had transmitted the information from the attorney general to the city attorney because "I believe it could have a bearing on things done in the future."

The mayor had independently sought an opinion from the attorney general on his power to appoint six members of the planning commission and to serve on the commission himself. Under Alabama law, the mayor, rather than the council, has the authority to appoint the planning commission and serves as a member or designates someone to serve in his or her place. The attorney general opined that Act 88–615 gave the council the authority to appoint the planning commission but that the mayor still should be a member. However, in the opinion letter, the attorney general added:

Although this office does not determine whether acts are constitutional, we note that generally speaking local acts, such as Act No. 88–615, that are in conflict with general law are unconstitutional. If Act No. 88–615 is constitutional, which is questionable, the provisions of Act No. 88–615 giving the council the appointing authority supersede the mayor's appointing authority.[7]

The mayor announced that he was calling a public meeting for early January 1990 "to find out how people feel about changing the city's form of government." In calling for the meeting, he stated: "I did not ask the attorney general to give an opinion on the form of government. I asked if I was eligible to sit on the city's planning commission and they sent back a letter saying the city's government may not be constitutional." The mayor stated that the city's form of government should not have been changed without a vote of the people, while admitting that he was "part of the problem" because he "was in office when the act was passed."

The city council responded by having the city attorney draft a bill to correct the constitutional problems of Act No. 88–615. The mayor was not satisfied with the council's bill because it did not put the question of form of government on a referendum for the voters to decide. The mayor requested the state legislative reference service to draft a bill for him that would require a referendum on the form of government. The mayor made his opposition to council-manager government known publicly:

> I don't like the present form of government we have. If we want to operate under the manager-council form, do what the code says—have a referendum.
> 11–43–20 gives a right to a city to hire a man if they want one. . . . If the people decide it, I'm just as happy as can be. We did the people wrong by sending that thing to Montgomery. A lot of us didn't understand exactly what we were doing.
> I want the mayor-council form of government with all its weaknesses and all its strong points.[8]

At the mayor's public meeting, 85 citizens attended, as well as the members of the city council and the city manager. Several of those in attendance complained about the sales tax and utility rate increases, as well as the $8 million bond issue. The mayor expressed his displeasure with the council-manager form of government once again and informed the crowd that he was planning to propose a referendum to let the citizens decide what form of government they wanted. He said a future council may not need a city manager: "If you look down the road to the 1992 election, we might get a bunch of Phi Beta Kappas up here and we might not need a city manager. The next council may want to work it that way." The council president told those in attendance at the mayor's meeting that the council had prepared a bill to correct what he termed a "typographical error in the act which refers to a non-existent section of the Alabama code."

The mayor also used the public forum as an opportunity to attack the city council. He said the council obviously agreed there was something wrong with the current bill because they are seeking to change it. However, he questioned the council "on just when they had instructed the city attorney to draft the new legislation. It wasn't done in a council meeting." The mayor urged the citizens to contact their council representatives and "let their feelings be known."

The following week, the city attorney presented to the city council his draft of a bill that would "clean-up" 88–615. The draft bill addressed the attorney general's concern that 88–615 was passed as local legislation and not as a general act that would apply to all cities of Daphne's size. The council also asked that the legislature include a provision that the form of government could not be changed within three years of its initial adoption. After three years, the form of government could be changed or amended when a "written petition executed by 10 percent of the number of those who voted in the last city election is submitted to the council with the proposed changes or amendments incorporated in the petition."

At the council meeting, the mayor objected to the council's proposed bill on two grounds. First, he thought the council should not be hasty in making the request to the legislature so that "citizens could have more time to study the proposed legislation." Second, he felt that the three-year moratorium on changing the form of government was not acceptable: "Three years to hold a referendum is a pretty good ways down the road." Since the council's term of office would be over at the end of three years, the council-manager advocates on the council apparently were interested in giving the form one full term of office to work. The mayor had announced his intention not to run for office after the current term, so he would have to serve the rest of his time as mayor under council-manager government—which was not appealing to him.

Within a week, the council members invited the state legislators from the area to meet with them to discuss their proposed bill that would correct the problems that the attorney general had identified with 88–615. The mayor told the legislators that he would insist a referendum be held in the near future because there had not been one when council-manager government was instituted. Forty pro-mayor residents also attended the meeting and presented the legislators with a petition with the names of 300 citizens who desired a referendum on the form of government. In an apparent victory for the mayor, "council members said that if the public wanted a referendum then they would agree with what the public wanted." However, the majority of the council felt that the referendum should be held at the time of the next council election in 1992.

The city manager, who had worked quietly with the council behind the scenes on the proposed legislation, then revealed that an audit of the city's Community Development Block Grant indicated that the mayor and his previous administration may have violated federal and state laws. The mayor immediately counterattacked in the press:

He (the mayor) went on to say how he had read about the city going to the grand jury, district attorneys, FBI's. "In all fairness I say let's do it expeditiously and find the culprits and let the others off the hook."

"It is understood the results of the audit were for your information not for anyone else but management," he said. "This shows the level of integrity that we have in this city hall."

The mayor said he was confident no investigation would find any violation of state law taking place during his previous administration. "You have put a stigma on a lot of innocent people."[9]

Meanwhile, the legislative delegation appeared reluctant to get in the middle of the dispute between the mayor and the council over the proposed changes, but eventually agreed to introduce the council's bill in the legislature. When the bill did not seem to be moving through the legislature, the council president wrote to the chairman of the Judiciary Committee to request the bill be placed

on the committee's agenda. In response to a request from the
mayor, the chairman of the committee notified the city that he had
scheduled a public hearing in Montgomery, a three-hour drive
from Daphne. The council president expressed his displeasure with
the chairman's decision to hold a public hearing in Montgomery:

> Given that seven public forums have been held regarding the annexa-
> tion, redistricting, and the form of government, the current city council
> believes that the mayor's request for another public forum at this point
> may be motivated by reasons other than notion of wanting the citizens to
> have additional input. As stated above, there have already been seven
> opportunities for public input and five of these opportunities were ar-
> ranged by (the mayor).
> As the legislative body of the city of Daphne, the city council is con-
> cerned that a public hearing at this point in the process might mean that
> this important legislation would not get before the House and the Senate
> during the current session.[10]

On the afternoon prior to the scheduled public hearing before
the Judiciary Committee in Montgomery, the city received word
from the committee secretary that the hearing had been canceled
by the chairman. Since there were only seven legislative days left
in the session, the mayor and city manager independently expressed
doubts that the bill would pass during the session. The city manager took the opportunity to criticize the state legislator who had
introduced the bill:

> We had four business hours notice. When the city clerk was notified by
> (the committee secretary), she confirmed that (our state legislator) knew
> about the cancellation. I would think out of courtesy we should have been
> notified by the local representative of the hearing cancellation.[11]

The city manager speculated that if the bill failed, the city council
would continue to operate under 88–615 that "the previous mayor
and council had passed." The mayor said he felt the council should
"go to court and get a judgment" on the legality of 88–615 if the
bill did not pass. Despite the council's subsequent compromise to
allow citizens to petition for a referendum on changing the form
of government 18 months prior to the next election, the bill died

in committee. The council's position in the earlier version of the bill allowed petitions only eight months prior to the 1992 election.

Following the failure of the legislature to enact the council's bill to correct 88–615, the mayor again went on the attack. At the next council meeting, he urged the council to seek a declaratory judgment in court on the legality of council-manager government because everything the council does "is suspect." The mayor added:

> One option is to go to the courts. And, really, you're not filing a suit against any one individual or group; just asking a court to make a determination.
>
> That's all I'm asking. Just ask a court to make a determination as to what form of government Daphne should be operating under.
>
> I personally think it would be better if the thing is cleared up as soon as possible. We've been going on since last October knowing there was something amiss.[12]

Within days after requesting the council to seek a declaratory judgment, the mayor announced that he had hired a lawyer to take the matter to court. He said it was "the hardest thing I've ever had to do," but that it must be done to remove the legal cloud over the city's form of government. The mayor's lawsuit had the unintended effect of halting a proposed $16 million bond issue for the utility board which was under orders from the state's environmental enforcement agency to make major improvements to its wastewater treatment facilities. The city's underwriter informed the council that the question of the form of government was making it very difficult to sell the city's bonds and he urged the council to have the matter resolved, preferably through the legislative process in the next session of the state legislature. Furthermore, the city attorney informed the council that he was in a difficult position because he "was appointed to serve the council and the mayor" and felt he could not serve both in this situation. He requested council approval to hire a law firm in Mobile to handle the council's defense against the mayor.

All the members of the council signed a letter to the mayor asking him to withdraw the court petition, but he informed the press that he had no intention of doing so. In a surprise move, the council filed a counterclaim against the mayor petitioning the court to remove the mayor from office and for him "to immediately return to the City of Daphne all benefits, including salary, received by him as a result of the office unlawfully held and to declare the office of mayor of the City of Daphne vacant" if the court decides that 88–615 was unconstitutional. The mayor angrily informed the council at the council meeting that "this does nothing to improve the relations between me and anybody that was a part of this action." The council president responded to the mayor by telling him that: "We asked you to sit down and negotiate and bring this to a speedy end but you sent a memo back saying this was not in the best interest of the city."

Meanwhile, the relationship between the city manager and the council was souring. The city manager had been instructed to identify possible parcels for the city to purchase on which to locate the new justice center. He had decided that the city should purchase a 45-acre site on the city's main highway that was selling for $3 million. The council's response was that the property was too expensive and suggested that he continue to look at other options. Unbeknownst to the council, the city manager had already contracted to purchase the property and had transferred $250,000 to an escrow account at a local bank. At a special called meeting to investigate the matter after word of it had spread to the council members, a council member confronted the city manager:

"Did we [the council] authorize money to be spent?"

"Negative," [the city manager] replied, stating that the money was in escrow pending the council's approval of the contract.

"I believe the funds were transferred September 7 and we weren't notified till last Monday night, and if I'm not mistaken, an agreement was made on September 12—we should have been notified when it happened, not a month later," [the council member] added.[13]

When the council declared its intent not to purchase the property, the city attorney advised the council that "the law is in our favor" since the council did not authorize the purchase of the property. The seller of the property insisted that he had a valid contract with the city and eventually sued the city. When he lost in lower court, he appealed the case to the Alabama Supreme Court. In 1992, the Supreme Court ruled in the city's favor, agreeing with the city's attorney's initial advice to the council that the city manager had no authority to purchase property for the city without the council's approval.

Following the meeting, the council held an executive session where the members decided to ask the city manager to resign. When the city manager refused to resign quietly at the council's request, the council called a special meeting one week later attended by an overflow crowd at the city hall. The council voted unanimously to ask for the city manager's resignation effective November 5, 1990. Following the meeting, at which no reasons were given for the request for the city manager's resignation, one council member stated that:

a lot of things that have happened in the city have happened because of (the city manager). Basically, the only thing I'll comment on is the justice center site. The fact that the council wasn't considered before funds were transferred and the fact that the city attorney wasn't included and no independent appraisal made of the property.[14]

The council president, who had been the city manager's primary supporter, stated that there were communication problems between the council and the city manager:

I just think that it's a breakdown in communication between the city council and the manager's office that has brought us to where we are tonight. Maybe not enough give and take in some situations. I want to say that there has not been anything illegal or unethical done by the city manager or his office. I think there have been severe errors in judgment by the city council and the city manager.[15]

At the regularly scheduled meeting on November 5, the council president read a letter from the city manager to the council in which he declined to resign unless certain "terms and conditions" were met by the council. The city manager requested to remain in his position until his successor was named and then remain on the payroll during a transition period with the new manager. Furthermore, he wanted the council to give him severance pay under the terms of his contract. The council's response to the letter was to dismiss the city manager effective immediately. The local newspaper described the scene:

> The motion (to dismiss the city manager) carried unanimously on a voice vote, which was followed by an outburst of cheering and clapping from those in the room.
>
> The outburst caused (the council president) to tell Daphne police (sergeant who was present) to escort the next person from the room who caused an uproar.[16]

In an interesting development, the council president turned over the gavel to the president pro tempore and moved that the council hire the city manager for up to four months until a replacement could be found. When the motion failed on a 4 to 3 voice vote, the city manager then asked the presiding officer if he could poll the council. The city manager, who had a stenographer present recording the meeting, was told that he could not poll the council.

On the same night the council members dismissed the city manager, they also appointed a committee to search for a temporary city manager. Within several days, the search committee interviewed three candidates for the position of temporary city manager and announced they would interview more applicants the following week. Seven additional candidates were interviewed in an open session of the search committee the next week. All the candidates were local businessmen except for one attorney. The search committee also agreed to begin advertising for a permanent city manager.

On November 19, two weeks after dismissing the city's first city manager, the council appointed a certified public accountant from a nearby town as the temporary city manager. The most noteworthy action of city manager II was his dismissal of the first city manager's comptroller who was caught mailing copies of her former boss' resume using the city's postage machine. Partly because of this action, city manager II developed a good relationship with the mayor, who later stated that he felt Daphne may have retained council-manager government had he been given the permanent position. City manager II was a candidate for the permanent position but was not chosen by the council despite receiving favorable response to his efforts while in the temporary position. The council president said that city manager II was not given the position on a permanent basis because he was "meager, meek and mild."

CITY MANAGER III ARRIVES FROM PENNSYLVANIA

Following several months of a nationwide search for a new city manager, the Daphne city council unanimously voted to hire its third city manager at an annual salary of $50,000. After interviewing four finalists from among over 100 applicants, the council decided to hire an experienced city manager from Pennsylvania. City manager III had been manager of a borough in Pennsylvania for the previous seven years and had earned a master of public administration degree from Pennsylvania State University. During his interview, city manager III stated that he felt he would bring with him "an extensive set of skills, experience, and knowledge to the job."

At the press conference announcing the hiring of city manager III, the council president stated that the new city manager "possessed the personality traits we were looking for, and everyone has agreed by their vote that they will support and work with him."

At the city council meeting on March 18, 1991, city manager III took the oath of office. At this same meeting, one of the council members moved that city manager II, who was the former interim manager, be appointed city treasurer on a "contractual basis" and that the finance committee be instructed to develop a contract to be approved by the council for his services as city treasurer. Interestingly, this vacancy was created by city manager II when he fired the comptroller five months earlier.

During this time, at the mayor's request, state legislators had introduced bills in the state legislature calling for a referendum to let the citizens of Daphne decide whether to retain council-manager government or to return to a mayor-council form prior to the next municipal election in August 1992. This legislation was passed by the legislature on July 17, 1991, and signed into law by the governor. Since the legislature did what the mayor advocated, the mayor's lawsuit against the city council was moot and was formally dismissed by a circuit court judge on December 18, 1991.

At a council meeting on August 19, 1991, the city council unanimously passed a resolution "to remain under the council-manager form of government . . . until a referendum can be held." All five citizens who spoke during the public hearing that evening were in favor of council-manager government. The referendum, later scheduled for February 11, 1992, would decide which form of government would take effect on October 5, 1992, when the new mayor and council members assumed office.

In an interview with the local press on the council-manager form of government and the upcoming referendum, the council president commented:

I think what we're operating under has worked extremely well. There have been some shakeups, but when you go from one form of government to another that's to be expected. It's had an opportunity to work and we know it will work. There are some people who have pointed to the fact that we've gone through several city managers, but I think the fact that we've gone through two or three managers in a period of time shows it's good. If you have a man who does not work out, the council can replace him if he's an employee, but if he's an elected official he's going to be there for four years.[17]

Unfortunately, the city council was not able to avoid controversy in the city in the months prior to the election. In December 1991, the city council voted to fire the popular city clerk, apparently on the recommendation of city manager III. Interestingly, her firing came about a month after the city council had voted to give her a $5,000 raise. One paper reported the incident by linking her termination with the question of the form of government:

Many [city] employees are worried that this is just the start of a massive shakeup by [city manager III]. . . .

The firing of the personable city clerk has also caused a lot of Daphne residents to begin thinking seriously about whether or not they want to keep the council-manager form of government. . . .

While [city manager III] says he is not a politician, one Daphne city councilman said the deal to fire [the city clerk] was well-orchestrated. . . .

"It was obvious [city manager III] had met or talked with at least five members of the Council. . . ."

"I didn't know they were going through with it until [the council president] made a motion to fire the city clerk."

For a while it looked as if the motion might die for lack of second until District 5 councilman . . . , who had tears in his eyes, finally seconded the motion.

With [the city clerk] calling the roll, the motion passed 5–2. . . . [18]

A forum, sponsored by the League of Women Voters and the Daphne Business Association, was held on January 29, 1992, to discuss the upcoming referendum. At the forum, city manager III spoke in favor of the council-manager form, saying it allowed for a professional administrator to run the city efficiently. The mayor said that the council-manager form created confusion for the residents over who was in charge of the city. He argued that the mayor-council form was more efficient.

During the forum, several local businessmen asked city manager III where the city purchases its supplies, accusing the city of making most of its purchases in Mobile. The owner of a local auto parts store was quoted as saying, "We are the ones who are buying the business licenses and are collecting the money this city uses to run itself. I believe we should have the first opportunity to bid on anything the city needs."

In response, city manager III said that the city's objective is to get the best price wherever that may be: "If it means going across the bridge (into Mobile), then I guess we'll go across the bridge." As he left the forum, one Daphne Business Association member said, "If I had been thinking about voting for the manager form of government tomorrow, that changed when I heard [the city manager's] talk."

One local publication reported that most residents were not aware of the issues surrounding the referendum and did not care about the form of government:

> In a very unscientific survey, conducted outside a local grocery store, ten registered voters were asked how they were going to vote in the February 11 referendum. Of the ten, six did not even know there was going to be a referendum. One said he was voting for the mayor, while the other three said they were not voting because it really didn't make any difference to them what form of government they were under.[19]

One Daphne resident said, "It's just not an issue that's going to excite a lot of people, especially the new residents who were annexed in."

At the January 22, 1992, city council meeting, the council passed a motion by a vote of 6 to 1 supporting council-manager government, and on February 3 passed a formal resolution by a vote of 5 to 1 to endorse the council-manager form. Although the mayor could not vote on the issue, he spoke in favor of the mayor-council form, arguing that under mayor-council government the voters directly select the administrator of the city. The council president spoke in favor of the council-manager form stating it "allows the elected officials of the council to control the administration of the city, but at the same time takes politics out of city operations."

On election day, Daphne residents chose to return to the mayor-council form of government by a 42-vote margin. Only 10 percent of the registered voters in Daphne went to the polls on February 11 to vote. The council president commented, "I'm disappointed that we're not going to retain one of the most progressive forms of government in the country. A lot of the disappointment is because there has been a lot of progress in the last four years under [the council-manager] system." Another member of the city council who also was a supporter of the council-manager form said that he felt that it wasn't right for 10 percent of the citizens to decide the form of government for the whole city of Daphne.

Several reasons were cited for the low voter turnout. According to city manager III, the main reason was apathy. He felt the community supported the council-manager system, and he thought it would have been a "no-brainer" for citizens to retain the system they had for the past three years. In an interview after he left Daphne, city manager III said he tried to stay out of the political arena over the issue of form of government, but regretted not having taken a more proactive approach to impress upon the residents the importance of the decision they were making.

A second reason for low voter turnout was confusion about the location of the new polling places, especially in the annexed areas of Daphne. One observer told the local press that many people, especially those who lived in Lake Forest, did not know where to cast their ballots. A third reason was that polls were open only from 8:00 A.M. to 6:00 P.M. Many residents of Daphne work in Mobile, making it difficult to vote before work begins at 8:00 A.M. or to have enough time to leave work to vote by 6:00 P.M. The city council had set the limited hours for polling places to be open.

A contributing cause of the rejection of council-manager govern-ment was the firing of the popular city clerk by the city manager. The local press quoted "a long-time Daphne political observer" as saying, "Sure there were a lot of people, especially in old Daphne [prior to annexation], who cast their vote for the mayor form of government because of [the mayor], but [city manager III] did not help insure his job security when he had [the city clerk] fired."

Approximately one week after the election, the city council passed an ordinance reducing the mayor's salary from $1,200 to $800 per month to be effective when the new mayor took office. The mayor vetoed the pay cut, stating that $800 per month is not sufficient for the new administrator of the city. A motion to over-ride the veto failed with only four votes in favor. The mayor told the press that $1,200 per month was not enough for a full-time mayor acting as the city's chief executive, especially in light of the $50,000 salary paid to the city manager.

On Friday night, March 20, 1992, city manager III was involved in a car accident in his municipal vehicle while driving home after having dinner with his wife. As a part of his contract, city manager III had "exclusive and unrestricted use of a city vehicle." He was arrested on DUI charges after one person was injured in the acci-dent and taken to the hospital, where she was treated and released. Several days later, city manager III told reporters that he had taken his family to dinner at a local restaurant. With his dinner, he con-sumed two or three beers and left the restaurant in the city vehicle. When he pulled onto the highway, he did not see the approaching vehicle. He also informed reporters that tests conducted after the accident by state troopers showed he was not intoxicated. When he was given a blood alcohol test two hours after the accident, the reading was 0.05 percent. At the time, Alabama law defined in-toxication at a 0.1 percent blood alcohol level or higher.

A special city council meeting was called to discuss a proposal to suspend city manager III until the DUI situation was resolved. The meeting was canceled due to a technicality in the manner in which it was called. The mayor said that any meeting held on the matter should not be an executive session, but should be open to the public and the media. City manager III commented, "The test showed I was not intoxicated. I think it [the meeting on suspen-sion] is totally premature."

At the next regular council meeting, the council voted 4 to 2 to delay action on the disciplinary action until the case was heard in court in April. In a written statement, one city council member told the media:

My major concern is one of basic judgment and lack of respect [city manager III] demonstrated by using the city vehicle after consuming alcohol. To me, waiting to see if he wins his court case for DUI is not the important issue here. The issue is whether [city manager III] is a responsible employee and upholds the best interest of the city of Daphne.[20]

After the arrest of the city manager, a local paper reported that city manager III was planning to discuss the mayor's violations of the legislative act governing the powers of the mayor at an upcoming city council meeting. At the meeting, city manager III accused the mayor of giving directives to city employees and requested the mayor be removed from office. "I'm quivering, I'm so scared," laughed the mayor. "This is just another one of his games to have the pressure taken off of him and his DUI case."

To make matters worse for the city council and the city manager, the former city clerk filed a $500,000 suit against the city, claiming that her civil rights were violated when she was fired without just cause and without a right to appeal. This case was later settled out of court.

At the regularly scheduled city council meeting in April 1992, the council rejected a motion to fire city manager III on a vote of 4 to 3, following a lengthy executive session. With the council president absent at the second city council meeting in April, the council reversed itself and voted 4 to 2 to fire city manager III. His DUI case had still not been heard in court. Upon hearing of the action that took place at the meeting, the council president called a special meeting to "make sure all the bases are covered." At a special called meeting three days later, the council decided to make the termination effective that evening, April 23, 1992. Also at the called meeting, the council unanimously voted to appoint the public works director as temporary city manager.

In a letter to the editor shortly thereafter, the council president stated:

One cannot help but wonder what some of this council would have done had they only a mayor to deal with and did not have a city manager to periodically terminate. Knowing they could not terminate the mayor would they have been able to put aside their minor differences and work together for the advancement of the city?[21]

The public works director served out the last few months of the term of office ending in October 1992 as interim city manager, but did not want to involve himself in the management of any departments but his own. According to the former mayor, the interim city manager called the mayor and asked him "to run things like he used to" because he did not want to become involved with the city council.

POSTSCRIPT

In the August 1992 election for mayor and council positions, the voters of Daphne rid themselves of the experiment in council-manager government and returned to mayor-council government. One of the councilors who had often opposed the city managers and council-manager government in general was elected mayor. Four other incumbents who ran for reelection were all defeated. When the new mayor and council were sworn into office on October 5, one of the first actions they took was to present the former mayor with a plaque and gift "in honor of his service to the city." After the presentation, the council then appointed the mayor to the utility board from which he was forced to resign two years later as part of a settlement with the district attorney over charges of misconduct by the board in polluting Mobile Bay.

ANALYSIS

Council-manager government stood little chance of succeeding in Daphne for numerous reasons. Political scientist James Svara described a state of "total conflict" where polarization, stalemate, subversion, and stonewalling are prevalent. To a large degree, Svara concluded that the structure of local government contributes to a conflictual environment. Fragmentation of authority is the single institutional factor most related to the creation of conflict.[22] In

Daphne, total conflict existed for the three and one-half years that the city operated under the council-manager form of government for the following reasons:

1. The careless manner in which the initial legislation (88–615) was crafted placed a cloud over the form of government from the beginning. Identifying its form of government as "mayor-council-manager" indicated the lack of understanding by the city councilors, state legislators, and attorneys who drafted and supported the initial legislation.

Instead of having the ability to prove that it was a viable option for governing, council-management government was the political target of the mayor during the full term of office because the enacting legislation was flawed. Eventually, the voters, in a very low turnout, rejected council-manager government and returned to the mayor-council form in hopes of eliminating the conflict.

2. Combining the form of government and the annexation questions on the same ballot confused many voters. An even more serious problem was the inability of the residents of Daphne to vote on either the annexation or the form of government. The people who lived in the areas to be annexed were given the power to choose whether they wanted to be part of Daphne and what form of government they would have. Daphne citizens not having the ability to vote on the form of government became the rallying cry of the mayor.

3. The structure of the government embodied some elements of separation of powers. It ensured failure by relegating the long-term mayor to a position of little formal authority. He was not a member of the council, nor did he have any administrative authority. The power to veto and access to the media assured the mayor of a platform to make his views known, however.

4. The actions of the city council in isolating the mayor even beyond what had been done legally added to the personal conflict between the mayor, council, and managers. The council removed the mayor from the planning commission, took away his power to appoint the planning commission, removed his name from the list of officials who could sign city checks, and excluded him from attending executive sessions of the council. When the mayor learned from the attorney general that 88–615 had constitutional problems, he was able to use the form of government question as

a vehicle for revenge. In an interview after he left office, the mayor indicated that he did not have a problem with the concept of a council-manager government and even believed that Daphne should once again give the form a chance to succeed.[23]

5. The first city manager seemed to go out of his way to take on political fights with the mayor, the council, and the state legislators. To a large degree, the council erred in limiting the search for its first manager to a few cities within the state and then choosing someone with no experience as a city manager. The reaction to his dismissal indicates that he was an unpopular figure within the community. His combative personality added to the state of total conflict in the city government. Both permanent city managers, who were dismissed by the council, were in constant conflict with the mayor.

Greg Protasel stated that in situations where the city manager is forced to take a more visible leadership role because of the lack of elected political leadership, it may cause legitimacy problems for the manager.[24] John Nalbandian argued that city managers are filling a policy void left by elected officials and sometimes they simply have a desire "to be in charge."[25] In Daphne, there is ample evidence that this was the case. Both of the permanent city managers assumed high profiles and spoke for the city on matters of policy. This was especially true of the first city manager, who even held press conferences prior to council meetings to discuss his proposals. His open sessions with citizens were designed to provide for him a high-profile policy position. One could easily conclude that city manager I transcended the bounds of ethical conduct for a city manager on numerous occasions, including the action that led to his termination. City manager III played a key role in the dismissal of the popular city clerk and recommended that the mayor be removed from office. There was little evidence that the council president or other council members were vocal on policy matters except in the constant conflict with the mayor.

Robert Montjoy and Douglas Watson pointed out that Alabama has not been a fertile ground for council-manager government.[26] To some degree, the failure of Daphne's officials to seek the advice of city managers in the state may have been based on their lack of information about the few cities that have adopted the form in the state. There obviously was not widespread understanding of or support for council-manager government in Daphne if the results of the second referendum are an indication. Very little effort was made to educate the citizens on how the form of government should work either before the first referendum or during its brief tenure in Daphne.

The mayor had been the undisputed head of the city government for a very long time before the change in 1989 to council-manager government. He was first elected to the city council in 1952 and had served as mayor for three terms prior to the one described here. Before 1989, his style was an informal one based on developing consensus among his friends on the city council, as demonstrated by the process of adoption of the district election map. The political culture of "old" Daphne conflicted with the tenets of professionalism embodied in city manager III. When city manager III developed a professional purchasing program based on low bids, the merchants in town were upset because they had never had any outside competition for the city's business under the old form of government. Those who had benefited under the "face-to-face, personalized" system of the mayor were ready allies of the mayor when he blamed council-manager government for their inability to do business with the city anymore.

The lessons to be learned from the Daphne case study for a city contemplating adoption of council-manager government are numerous. At the very minimum, a community must demonstrate understanding of the system that it is adopting and be committed to a different way of doing business. The structure of the government should be one where conflict is minimized and the legal basis is very carefully researched. Also, the city council should choose the first manager very carefully through the advice of officials from other cities or institutes of government located at state universities. Most importantly, the elected officials must provide political leadership so that the manager is not forced to be the political head of the local government.

NOTES

1. Act No. 88–615 of the Alabama Legislature, dated May 18, 1988.
2. Interview with A. Victor Guarisco, July 28, 1995, Daphne, Alabama.

3. Jean Richmond, "No Map for Daphne—City Council Considers Repealing Annexation," *Baldwin Press Register,* November 9, 1988, p. 3.

4. JoAnn Collins, "New Voting Procedures Set for Daphne Elections," *Baldwin Press Register,* April 3, 1989, pp. 1–2.

5. Ibid., p. 2.

6. Robert S. Montjoy and Douglas J. Watson, "Within-Region Variation in Acceptance of Council-Manager Government: Alabama and the Southeast," *State and Local Government Review* 25, no. 1 (Spring 1993): 19–27.

7. Letter from Attorney General Don Siegelman to Mayor A. Victor Guarisco, October 19, 1989.

8. Susan French Cone, "Guarisco: Make City Manager Job an Optional One," *Baldwin Press Register,* January 2, 1990, pp. 1–2.

9. "Mayor Disputes Recent Newspaper Stories on City Audit," *Eastern Shore News,* February 8, 1990, pp. 1, 8.

10. Susan French Cone, "Public Hearing Scheduled for Daphne Bill," *Baldwin Press Register,* March 25, 1990, pp. 1–2.

11. Susan French Cone, "Daphne Bill May Die in Committee," *Baldwin Press Register,* March 28, 1990, pp. 1, 4.

12. Susan French Cone, "Guarisco: Court Should Decide Constitutionality of Daphne Government," *Baldwin Press Register,* April 18, 1990, p. 2.

13. Cathy Barnett, "Daphne Rejects Justice Center Land Agreement," *Baldwin Press Register,* October 23, 1990, p. 3.

14. Susan French Cone and Cathy Barnett, "Council Asks Arnold to Quit," *Baldwin Press Register,* October 30, 1990, pp. 1–2.

15. Ibid.

16. "Daphne City Council Terminates City Manager—Begins Search for Temporary Replacement," *Eastern Shore News,* November 10, 1990, pp. 1, 9.

17. Guy Busby and Susan Godwin, "Daphne Gearing Up for Vote," *Baldwin Press Register,* August 4, 1991, p. 1.

18. "Lapeze Firing Leaves Many Employees Thinking *Could I Be Next?*" *Eastern Shore News,* December 21, 1991, pp. 4–5.

19. "Daphne Voters to Go to Polls Feb. 11," *Eastern Shore News,* January 25, 1992, p. 5.

20. Guy Busby, "Daphne Delays Action on City Manager," *Baldwin Press Register,* March 31, 1992, p. 1.

21. Marvin P. Ussery, "Herman's Leadership Will Be Missed," *Baldwin Press Register* [Letters to the Editor], April 26, 1992.

22. James H. Svara, *Official Leadership in the City* (London: Oxford University Press, 1990), pp. 30–31.

23. Interview with A. Victor Guarisco, July 28, 1995, Daphne, Alabama.

24. Greg J. Protasel, "Abandonments of the Council-Manager Plan—A New Institutionalist Perspective," in H. George Frederickson, ed., *Ideal and Practice in Council-Management Government* (Washington, DC: International City Management Association, 1989), pp. 28–29.

25. John Nalbandian, *Professionalism in Local Government* (San Francisco: Jossey-Bass Publishers, 1991), pp. 58–59.

26. Montjoy and Watson, "Within-Region Variation in Acceptance of Council-Manager Government," pp. 19–27.

8

Epilogue

DOUGLAS J. WATSON

In the opening chapter, three scenarios in local government were identified that produced innovation. One was the need to overcome adversity. In a recent *Governing* magazine article, H. George Frederickson noted that many times innovation takes place even in "harsh circumstances." A situation has become so intolerable that the public or elected officials are clamoring for change. The public administrator realizes that the adverse situation must be addressed and he or she develops a response that will solve the problem by changing the way the government approaches it. In these harsh circumstances, there is consensus for the innovative solution even among political enemies because the situation has become intolerable.

The second scenario is the existence within local governments of exceptional people, both elected and appointed. The elected officials expect the appointed managers to be innovative and are supportive of them when they propose new and better ways of delivering services to the community. Many innovations are new directions for the local government into areas that are not traditionally delivered by the government. Oftentimes, local governments that display this condition are ones that are stable, with a minimum of conflict among the elected officials and between the elected officials and the public administrators. The organizational culture encourages managers to be innovative by being open and supportive of new ideas.

The third scenario, while most likely to be found in stable and supportive organizations, is that of organizations seizing opportunities when they appear. Sometimes innovative ideas will not be accepted because they are suggested at the wrong time or under the wrong circumstances. It is important for elected and appointed officials to understand when the circumstances are right for innovation and to seize the opportunity to gain acceptance for the new idea. Generally, unless the government is facing serious adversity, support for innovations has to be gradually developed.

In the case studies that were presented in the earlier chapters, evidence of the importance of all three scenarios can be found. Oftentimes, more than one of the scenarios will be involved in the production of an innovation. Furthermore, it may not be a simple matter of determining which of the three scenarios was the most important in creating the innovation. For example, in describing the development of the stormwater utility in Martin County, Ronald W. McLemore and T. Duncan Rose, III identify all three scenarios. The county was clearly facing a crisis in managing its water resources because of the rapid development of the past two decades. A tropical storm and a hurricane illustrated the failure of the current stormwater system to the community in recent months.

In addition, the authors describe a capable staff that involved outside expert help in the development of the stormwater utility. At each step of the process, the staff involved the community and the county commission and sought input from groups that had special interests in the solution to the stormwater problem. Lastly, the county realized that there was support in the community to take action to solve the problem, even if it involved imposing an assessment on the residents.

The insurance crisis and the creation of the risk management function in Tallahassee also involve all three scenarios, according to Steven A. Reeves' case study. The city staff did not allow internal "turf" concerns to stand in the way of the innovative solution that they had created to address the adverse situation the city faced. The city manager agreed that risk management should remain in the treasurer clerk's office, even though he realized that many of the risk management functions are essentially management in nature. The city council was very supportive of the staff recommendation to move from the traditional way of dealing with risk through insurance, even though that is the way the city "had always done it."

In the Auburn public safety case studies, Cortez Lawrence describes public managers who wanted to find a more efficient way of delivering fire and emergency medical services to the community. It is obvious from the case study that the organizational culture was supportive of innovation even in the face of employee opposition to the changes. The Auburn public administrators also seized the opportunity to implement their innovations at the right time. For example, both of these innovations were accomplished after senior chiefs of police and fire retired and after the city had been involved in litigation with some of the employees. In addition, factors in the community, such as the presence of many talented university students who were interested in the firefighter program, presented an opportunity to innovate.

Robert J. Juster's study of the change from prescriptive to performance zoning also illustrates strong and supportive political leadership, careful attention to community involvement, and a commitment to innovation based on a belief that it would benefit the community. In that case, members of the planning commission and the city council faced strong public opposition from neighborhood groups whose members attended public meetings for months. While the growth of the community had clearly outpaced the ability of the old zoning ordinance to control it in an orderly manner, the city was not facing an immediate crisis. Rather, the political and appointed leaders of the community realized that the Auburn 2000 process had given them an opportunity to address the development needs in the community in a comprehensive way. Instead of shrinking from that opportunity, they persevered in the face of strong community opposition.

Four of the case studies have several elements in common. First, they are all success stories. Second, they all describe how elected and appointed officials in organizations worked together to support innovative solutions to pressing problems. Third, they all involve political and/or community support that was carefully nurtured to support the innovation. Fourth, the four studies describe talented and dedicated public administrators who wanted to serve the public more efficiently and effectively. None were given large bonuses for their ideas, unlike what their counterparts in the private sector may have received. And fifth, all the innovations were implemented successfully.

By contrast, the attempt to bring an innovative form of local government to the small city of Daphne was an utter failure in every regard. While the city council seized an opportunity to innovate, they made no attempt to involve their constituents in the decision. The residents of Daphne were not even allowed to vote on the form of government at the time residents of the areas to be annexed were deciding not only whether they wanted to be part of Daphne but also what form of government the city would have. The lessons in the Daphne case are abundant for how not to develop and implement an innovative approach to solving community problems. Conflict was pervasive in the city government even when some of the characters changed. No attempt was made to find common ground between the mayor and the council on any issues. The conflict went to the extreme of the two sides filing suit against each other. The city managers added to the conflict by their actions, as described in the study. Unlike the other case studies, there was no capable professional management in place and no supportive environment for innovation. The adversity was created from within the organization, rather than the organization coming together to develop a solution to the adversity that it faced.

CONCLUSION

Local governments have a unique opportunity to be innovative for several reasons. One is that local governments are very close to the problems in their communities. Unlike other levels of government, local officials have the chance to see and hear the problems as they develop. A second reason local governments can be innovative is that there are so many of them doing basically the same things. Each community serves as a laboratory for innovation. Unique circumstances allow local governments to solve problems and develop solutions in different ways. Unlike private companies that have to guard their new ideas, local governments take pride in sharing their innovations with other communities. A third reason is that most elected officials on the local level run for office because they care about their communities and believe that they can improve them. The last reason is that the level of competence and expertise found among local public administrators has greatly increased over the past several decades. Local public administrators are better trained than they have ever been and are anxious to work for organizations that allow them to use their talents.

Selected Bibliography

Babcock, Richard F. and Charles L. Siemon. *The Zoning Game Revisited.* Cambridge, MA: Lincoln Institute of Land Policy, 1985.

Banovetz, James M. *Managing Local Government: Cases in Decision Making.* Washington, DC: International City Management Association, 1990.

Bryson, John M. and William D. Roering. "Initiation of Strategic Planning by Governments." *Public Administration Review* 48, no. 6 (November/December 1988): 995–1004.

Crawford, Clan, Jr. *Strategy and Tactics in Municipal Zoning,* 2nd ed. Englewood Cliffs, NJ: Prentice-Hall, 1979.

Donahue, John D. *The Privatization Decision: Public Ends, Private Means.* New York: Basic Books, 1989.

Dittmar, Mary Jane. "Ownership of the Fire Service." *Fire Engineering* (September 1992): 81–94.

Dunlap, T. Phillip, Bettye B. Burkhalter, Douglas J. Watson, and Jacki Fitzpatrick. "Reshaping the Local Economy Through a Revolving Loan Fund (RLF) Project in an Entrepreneurial City." *Economic Development Quarterly* 9, no. 1 (February 1995): 74–79.

Ehrenhalt, Alan. "Can Government's Arteries Be Unclogged?" *Governing* (February 1994): 6–7.

Harkness, Peter A. "The Impulse to Innovate." *Governing* (October 1992): 34–35.

Heilman, John G. and Gerald W. Johnson. *The Politics and Economics of Privatization.* Tuscaloosa, AL: The University of Alabama Press, 1992.

Henkoff, Ronald. "Some Hope for Troubled Cities." *Fortune* (September 9, 1991): 121–128.

International Association of Fire Fighters. *Emergency Medical Services: A Guide Book for Fire-Based Systems.* Washington, DC: International Association of Fire Fighters, 1995.

Johnson, Gerald W. and Douglas J. Watson. "Privatization: Provision or Production of Services: Two Case Studies." *State and Local Government Review* 23, no. 2 (Spring 1991): 82–89.

Kellar, Elizabeth K. *Managing with Less.* Washington, DC: International City Management Association, 1979.

Kendig, Lane. *Performance Zoning.* Chicago: Planners Press, American Planning Association, 1980.

Kettl, Donald F. *Sharing Power: Public Governance and Private Markets.* Washington, DC: The Brookings Institute, 1993.

Kleem, John. "Innovation: The Perceptions of an Australian Local Government Manager." *Public Management* (May 1989): 7–10.

Lampkin, Linda and Margaret Pennington. "Should Private Companies Provide State Services?" In Howard R. Balanoff, ed., *Annual Editions, Public Administration,* 3rd ed. Guilford, CT: Dushkin Publishing Company, 1993, pp. 141–142.

Lawrence, Cortez. "Company Staffing: The Proof Is in Your Numbers." *Fire Engineering* (April 1995): 61–64.

Mandelker, Daniel R. *Land Use Law,* 2nd ed. Charlottesville, VA: The Michie Company, 1988.

Montjoy, Robert S. and Douglas J. Watson. "Within-Region Variation in Acceptance of Council-Manager Government: Alabama and the Southeast." *State and Local Government Review* 25, no. 1 (Spring 1993): 19–27.

———. "A Case for Reinterpreted Dichotomy of Politics and Administration as a Professional Standard in Council-Manager Government." *Public Administration Review* 55, no. 3 (May/June 1995): 231–239.

Morrison, Richard. *Manning Levels for Engine and Ladder Companies in Small Fire Departments.* Emmitsburg, MD: National Fire Academy (unpublished), 1990.

Nalbandian, John. *Professionalism in Local Government.* San Francisco: Jossey-Bass Publishers, 1991.

National Academy of Public Administration. *Privatization: The Challenge* to *Public Management*. Washington, DC: National Academy of Public Administration, 1989.

Osborne, David. "The Power of Outdated Ideas." *Governing* (December 1992): 61.

Osborne, David and Ted Gaebler. *Reinventing Government*. Reading, MA: Addison-Wesley Publishing Company, 1992.

Pennisi, Sam. "Local Government and Innovation." *Public Management* (May 1989): 5–6.

Protasel, Greg J. "Abandonments of the Council-Manager Plan—A New Institutionalist Perspective." In H. George Frederickson, ed., *Ideal and Practice in Council-Management Government*. Washington, DC: International City Management Association, 1989.

Rosen, Ellen Doree. *Improving Public Sector Productivity: Concepts and Cases*. Newbury Park, CA: Sage Publications, 1993.

Savas, E. S. *Privatization: The Key to Better Government*. Chatham, NJ: Chatham House Publishers, 1987.

Sensenbrenner, Joseph. "Quality for Cities." *Nation's Business* (October 1991): 61–62.

Steinbach, Carol. *Innovations in American Government*. New York: Ford Foundation, 1995.

Svara, James H. *Official Leadership in the City*. London: Oxford University Press, 1990.

Svara, James H. and Associates. *Facilitative Leadership in Local Government*. San Francisco: Jossey-Bass Publishers, 1994.

Sylvester, Kathleen. "Risk and the Culture of Innovation." *Governing* (October 1992): 46–50.

Ukeles, Jacob B. *Doing More with Less*. New York: AMACOM, 1982.

Walters, Jonathan. "Reinventing the Federal System." *Governing* (January 1994): 49–53.

———. "Can Innovation Be Taught?" *Governing* (November 1993): 52–57.

Watson, Douglas J. *The New Civil War: Government Competition for Economic Development*. Westport, CT: Praeger Publishers, 1995.

Watson, Douglas J., Robert J. Juster, and Gerald W. Johnson. "Institutionalized Use of Citizen Surveys in the Budgetary and Policymaking Processes: A Small City Case Study." *Public Administration Review* 51, no. 3 (May/June 1991): 232–239.

Wheeland, Craig A. "A Profile of a Facilitative Mayor: Mayor Betty J. Rhea of Rock Hill, South Carolina." In James H. Svara and Associates, *Facilitative Leadership in Local Government*. San Francisco: Jossey-Bass Publishers, 1994, pp. 136–159.

Index

About the Editor
and Contributors

DOUGLAS J. WATSON is the City Manager of Auburn, Alabama. Dr. Watson received his undergraduate degree in Government and Politics from the University of Maryland, his Master of Public Administration from the University of Georgia, and his Ph.D. from Auburn University. He has won numerous awards, including the L. P. Cookingham Award for Career Development from the International City–County Management Association. He is a Visiting Associate Professor in the Master of Public Administration program at Auburn University, and has published several books and numerous articles in the public administration field, including *Politics of Redistributing Urban Aid* (Praeger, 1994) and *The New Civil War: Government Competition for Economic Development* (Praeger, 1995). He continues to be active in researching and writing in the area.

T. PHILLIP DUNLAP is the Economic Development Director of the City of Auburn, Alabama. In addition to serving as a department head, he also serves as the secretary/treasurer to the Industrial Development Board, Auburn Redevelopment Authority, and the Auburn Center for Developing Industries, which operates the city's business incubator facility. Mr. Dunlap has an undergraduate degree from the University of Alabama, Birmingham (UAB) and has completed additional graduate work at UAB and Jacksonville State University.

WENDY L. HASSETT is currently the Assistant to the City Manager in Auburn, Alabama. She has a background in housing and economic development. She received her undergraduate degree in Business Management in 1991 and her Master of Public Administration degree from Auburn University in March 1993.

ROBERT J. JUSTER was the Director of Planning and Community Development for the City of Auburn, Alabama, from 1990 until he retired in 1996. Previously he was Planning Director for Chattanooga, Tennessee; Director of the Birmingham Regional Planning Commission in Birmingham, Alabama; and Director of Planning for an engineering firm based in Columbia, South Carolina. He has taught Urban Planning at the University of Alabama in Birmingham and the University of Mississippi. Presently he is a Visiting Professor of Architecture at Auburn University and teaches in the Graduate Program in Community Planning. He has an M.P.A. from the John F. Kennedy School of Government at Harvard University and a Ph.D. in Political Science from Vanderbilt University.

CORTEZ LAWRENCE is currently the Deputy Director of the Public Safety Department for the City of Auburn, Alabama. He has earned J.D. and M.P.A. degrees and is a Ph.D. candidate. Mr. Lawrence is active on the National Fire Protection Association Instructor Qualifications Committees and International Association of Fire Chiefs Accreditation Committees. He is an adjunct instructor at the National Fire Academy, a visiting lecturer at Auburn University, a Certified Emergency Manager, and the author and presenter of several articles and seminars on public safety matters and general public administration.

RONALD W. McLEMORE is the City Manager of Winter Springs, Florida. Mr. McLemore has 25 years of public service experience, including executive positions in municipal, county, and state government, and consulting engagements with over 70 governmental units. Mr. McLemore has published in numerous areas of local government and won several awards for administrative excellence. Mr. McLemore was awarded his Bachelor's Degree from Georgia Southern University in 1969 and Master's Degree from the University of Georgia in 1972.

STEVEN A. REEVES is the Director of Human Resource Management for the City of Auburn, Alabama. Prior to this appointment, he served as that city's Risk Manager. His professional background also includes state and local government consulting service. He holds a Master of Public Administration degree from Auburn University.

T. DUNCAN ROSE, III is President of Government Systems Group L.C., a recently formed local government–oriented management services company specializing in developing non–ad valorem assessment systems, especially stormwater utilities. Mr. Rose received his undergraduate degree in Economics/Management from Grove City College, Master of Science in Planning from University of Tennessee, and Master of Public Administration from Ohio State University.

ISBN 0-275-95515-X

EAN

9 780275 955151

90000>

HARDCOVER BAR CODE